LAW ENFORCEMENT AGENCIES

U.S. MARSHALS

Bomb Squad

Border Patrol

Crime Lab

Drug Enforcement Administration

Federal Bureau of Investigation

Interpol

Los Angeles Police Department

New York Police Department

The Secret Service

SWAT Teams

The Texas Rangers

U.S. Marshals

LAW ENFORCEMENT AGENCIES

U.S. MARSHALS

Michael Newton

U.S. MARSHALS

Chelsea House
An imprint of Infobase Learning
132 West 31st Street
New York NY 10001

Library of Congress Cataloging-in-Publication Data

Newton, Michael, 1951-
U.S. marshals / Michael Newton.
p. cm. — (Law enforcement agencies)
Includes bibliographical references and index.
ISBN-13: 978-1-60413-627-2 (hardcover : alk. paper)
ISBN-10: 1-60413-627-8 (hardcover : alk. paper)
1. United States. Marshals Service. 2. United States marshals.
3. Law enforcement—United States. I. Title.
HV8144.M37N49 2011 363.28'20973—dc22
2010038195

Chelsea House books are available at special discounts when purchased in bulk quantities for businesses, associations, institutions, or sales promotions. Please call our Special Sales Department in New York at (212) 967-8800 or (800) 322-8755.

You can find Chelsea House on the World Wide Web at http://www.chelseahouse.com

Text design and composition by Erika K. Arroyo
Cover design by Keith Trego
Cover printed by Bang Printing, Brainerd, Minn.
Book printed and bound by Bang Printing, Brainerd, Minn.
Date printed: February 2011

Printed in the United States of America

10 9 8 7 6 5 4 3 2 1

This book is printed on acid-free paper.

All links and Web addresses were checked and verified to be correct at the time of publication. Because of the dynamic nature of the Web, some addresses and links may have changed since publication and may no longer be valid.

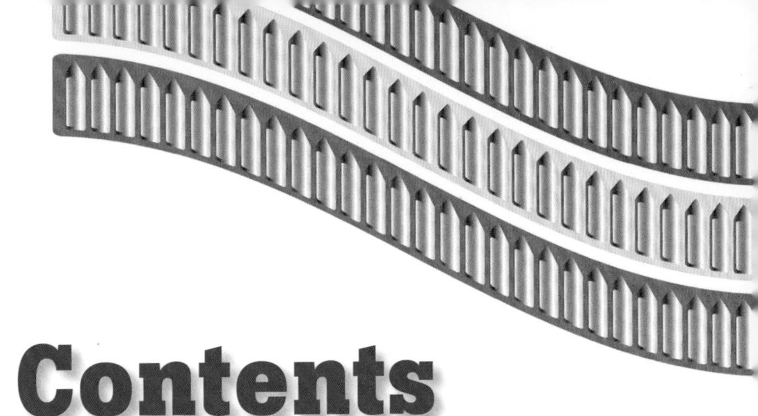

Contents

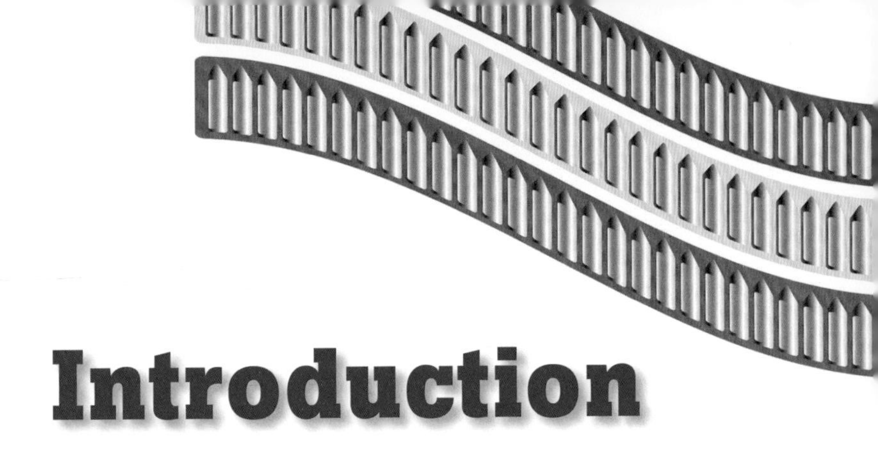

Introduction

Fighting crime in the United States is a complex procedure, involving a nationwide network of federal, state, and local law enforcement agencies, prosecutors, and courts. In 2004—the last year with comprehensive statistics available—836,787 sworn law enforcement officers served 17,928 separate agencies from coast to coast. Fifty-two of those have headquarters in Washington, D.C.[1]

Some national agencies, such as the Federal Bureau of Investigation (FBI), the U.S. Secret Service, and the Drug Enforcement Administration (DEA), are world-famous. Others—such as the Library of Congress Police, the National Institutes of Health Police, and the Smithsonian Institution's National Zoological Park Police—remain largely unknown to most Americans outside their limited jurisdictions.

The U.S. Marshals Service is America's oldest and most versatile federal law enforcement agency. Created by Congress in September 1789—76 years before the Secret Service, 119 years before the FBI, and 184 years before the DEA—the service began as a team of 13 handpicked officers. Today, it includes 4,901 employees dispersed among 94 judicial districts, with 218 sub-offices and three foreign field offices. Of those employees, 94 are U.S. marshals (one for each of America's federal court districts), while 3,320 are deputy U.S. marshals or criminal investigators.[2]

The original responsibility of U.S. marshals—and still a primary concern today—was maintaining the security of federal courts. Until the Secret Service was created, U.S. marshals also were the country's frontline of defense against counterfeit money. They enforced federal liquor laws until the 1920s, while pursuing wartime spies and saboteurs. Today, their duties include housing federal prisoners prior to trial and transporting convicts to federal prisons, operating the federal Witness

America's oldest federal law enforcement agency, the U.S. Marshals was created in 1789 to provide security for federal courts and enforce federal liquor laws. *(Corbis)*

Security Program, managing assets seized from federal offenders, investigating sex offender registration violations, and apprehending federal fugitives. U.S. marshals arrest more fugitives from justice than all other federal agencies combined—more than 36,000 in 2008 alone.[3]

U.S. Marshals tracks the history of America's first national police force and examines its duties in detail.

Chapter 1, "U.S. Marshals," provides an overview of the U.S. Marshals Service and its various present-day duties.

Chapter 2, "Early Marshals," details the agency's creation in 1789, when President George Washington appointed the first 13 U.S. marshals, examining some of the diverse and colorful characters who wore a marshal's badge.

Chapter 3, "Counterfeiting," reviews the pursuit of counterfeiters by U.S. marshals, prior to creation of the U.S. Secret Service in 1865.

Chapter 4, "Court Security," examines the role of U.S. marshals in supervising and protecting federal courts since passage of the 1789 Judiciary Act.

Chapter 5, "Difficult Tasks," surveys the role of U.S. marshals in supervising federal executions, enforcing the Fugitive Slave Act of 1850, pursuing bootleggers before the creation of the Treasury Department's Prohibition Bureau, and suppressing violent civil disorders.

Chapter 6, "Marshals in War and Peace," covers the defense of America from foreign enemies and homegrown subversives, from the War of 1812 through Operation Desert Storm and the 21st-century war on terrorism.

Chapter 7, "Witness Security Program (WITSEC)," describes operations of the Witness Security Program from its inception in 1971 to the present.

Chapter 8, "Dangerous Duty," reviews case histories of the 235 U.S. marshals killed in the line of duty since 1794.

Chapter 9, "Most Wanted," describes the role of U.S. marshals in pursuing federal fugitives, including sting operations and the Fugitive Safe Surrender program, with profiles of the top fugitives presently at large.

U.S. Marshals

Chicago, Illinois

Harry Belluomini spent 32 years as an officer of the Chicago Police Department before he joined the U.S. Marshals Service in 1989. At an age when most lawmen retire, he had started a second career. With fellow Deputy Marshal Roy Frakes, Belluomini was assigned to the Everett McKinley Dirksen United States Courthouse, located on South Dearborn Street in Chicago. They reported for work as usual on July 20, 1992.

That Monday was a normal day, until bank robber Jeffrey Erickson slipped out of his handcuffs, overpowered a guard in the courthouse basement, and seized her revolver. Deputy Marshal Frakes confronted Erickson before he could flee the basement, and died on the spot as Erickson shot him twice from close range. Harry Belluomini was close behind his partner, exchanging fire with Erickson and wounding the gunman before two more bullets ended Belluomini's life. Disabled and bleeding, aware of the other lawmen rushing to surround him, Erickson saved a final shot for himself.[1]

While survivors and colleagues mourned the slain officers, other marshals investigated Erickson's escape. They learned that he had bought a handcuff key from fellow bank bandit Robert Burke, using it to ditch his "bracelets" in the courthouse basement. U.S. marshals later traced Burke to England, where he was arrested by British police and extradited to Chicago for trial on charges of aiding a federal prisoner's escape. Jurors convicted him in September 2003, and he received a 20-year prison term.[2]

In January 2007 the Seventh Circuit Court of Appeals upheld Burke's conviction but urged Judge Rebecca Pallmeyer to consider a lighter sentence. Nine months later, Judge Pallmeyer repeated the original sentence: 20 years in prison for aiding an escape that cost the lives of two deputy U.S. marshals. The Seventh Circuit affirmed that sentence on June 11, 2008.[3]

ANYTIME, ANYWHERE

U.S. marshals describe their badge as "America's star," a double reference to the age of their service and the broad range of their modern duties.[4] Established as the first federal law enforcement agency in 1789, with 13 officers, today the U.S. Marshals Service has 4,942 employees. Director John Clark and Deputy Director Brian Beckwith run the agency from headquarters in Arlington, Virginia. Nationwide, each of America's 94 federal court districts has its own U.S. marshal, with 3,345 deputy marshals and criminal investigators supported by 1,503 administrative employees and detention enforcement officers.[5]

All but one of the 94 U.S. marshals are appointed by the president to four-year terms of service, with advice and consent of the U.S. Senate. The sole exception, who serves in the U.S. Virgin Islands, is appointed by the U.S. attorney general. Federal law (Section 561 of Title 28, U.S. Code) specifies that candidates for U.S. marshal must have college training and significant experience in the administration of justice, including four years of command-level law enforcement management duties, experience in coordinating operations between different police agencies, and experience with local, state, or federal court systems, including protection of court personnel, jurors, and witnesses. No age limits are specified, but candidates must be capable of "forceful and vigorous activity."[6]

Once selected and confirmed, U.S. marshals perform a range of duties unrivaled by those of any other federal law enforcement agents.

JUDICIAL SECURITY

Created more than 220 years ago to ensure the security of America's federal courts, the U.S. Marshals Service continues that work in the

THE "THREE GUARDSMEN"

Oklahoma Territory was a no-man's land of crime between its creation in May 1890 and its statehood in November 1907. "Hanging Judge" Isaac Parker administered the district from his federal court in Fort Smith, Arkansas, aided by U.S. Marshal Evett Nix, but the dangerous work of arresting outlaws fell to a trio of deputy U.S. marshals widely known as the "Three Guardsmen": Chris Madsen (1851–1944), Henry "Heck" Thomas (1850–1912), and Ben Tilghman (1854–1924). Together, they jailed some 300 felons and killed several more. Members of the bank-and-train-robbing Dalton Gang named Thomas as their main reason for leaving Oklahoma; members of the gang were later massacred at Coffeyville, Kansas, in October 1892. Between 1894 and 1896 the Three Guardsmen also wiped out most of Bill Doolin's bank-robbing gang.

Madsen and Thomas retired from the U.S. Marshals Service in 1905 but remained in law enforcement—Madsen serving as chief of police in Oklahoma City, while Thomas held the same position in Lawton, Oklahoma, until his death from Bright's disease (a kidney disorder) in 1912. Tilghman retired in 1910 and was elected to Oklahoma's state senate, and then replaced Chris Madsen as Oklahoma City's police chief in 1911. In 1915 Tilghman wrote, directed, and starred in a movie, *The Passing*

21st century. Its Judicial Security Division (JSD)—which established the National Center for Judicial Security in March 2007—anticipates and intercepts any threats to the safe and orderly operation of federal courts nationwide, as well as in the U.S. Virgin Islands, Puerto Rico, and on the Western Pacific island of Guam. A deputy assistant director leads the JSD from headquarters in Arlington.

Within the JSD resides an Office of Protective Intelligence, equipped with officers who investigate more than 1,000 threats against federal courts and judges each year. Each threat, however far-fetched or bizarre, must be taken seriously and examined for potential danger. The Office *of the Oklahoma Outlaws,* which dramatized the work of the Three Guardsmen. Chris Madsen and Marshal Evett Nix portrayed themselves in that film.

Madsen tried to join the U.S. Army in April 1917, when the United States entered World War I, but recruiters rejected him due to his age. Seven years later, Bill Tilghman accepted a job as marshal in Cromwell, Oklahoma, where bootleggers and other criminals had set up shop. He had repeated arguments with Wiley Lynn, a corrupt federal Prohibition agent who released many prisoners jailed by Tilghman. On October 31, 1924, Lynn shot and killed Tilghman in a street fight. Jurors acquitted him of murder after several frightened witnesses left town, but he lost his government job. One month after Tilghman's murder, arsonists—allegedly led by Chris Madsen—burned most of Cromwell to the ground. State police declined to investigate the fire.

Wiley Lynn ran out of luck on July 17, 1932, when he was killed in another shootout with police that also claimed the lives of Agent Crockett Long, from the Oklahoma State Bureau of Investigation, and an unarmed bystander. Two other bystanders were also wounded in the battle. Chris Madsen lived on for another 12 years, dying at age 93 on January 9, 1944.

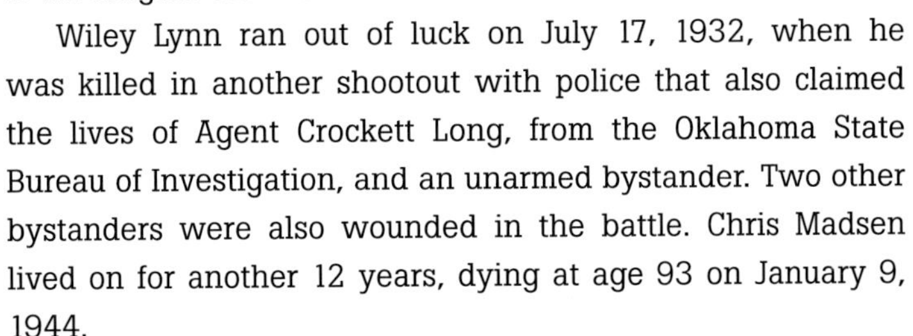

of Protective Operations carries out investigations and provides tight security at more than 400 federal court facilities; more than 2,000 sitting judges and some 5,250 other employees work at these locations.[7]

The work does not end there. The Office of Court Security supervises all assigned federal court security officers, conducting an average 5,000 screenings on new applicants and serving officers per year.[8] A separate Office of Security Contracts is responsible for purchasing security equipment, hiring additional personnel as needed, and maintaining a sophisticated Home Intrusion Detection System to safeguard federal judges during their off-duty hours.

U.S. Marshal Nicholas Gustin stands with a weapon in front of the federal courthouse in Seattle. *(AP Photo/Elaine Thompson)*

Once surveillance and weapons-screening equipment is tested and approved for purchase, installation falls to the Office of Security Systems. Meanwhile, the Office of Financial Management keeps tabs on the expense of court security measures, dispensing payment to vendors and contractors outside of the U.S. Marshals Service from a budget that totaled $312 million in 2007. In 2009, the last year with figures available, the office requested $933 million from Congress.[9]

Involvement with federal courts does not end for U.S. marshals at the courthouse steps, or at the homes of sitting judges. Marshals also serve as the enforcement arm of federal courts, beginning with service of process—writs, warrants, subpoenas, injunctions, and other orders issued by federal judges nationwide. Those orders involve both criminal and civil cases and may send deputy marshals on globe-trotting visits to distant countries.

Once a trial concludes, U.S. marshals are responsible for conducting the public sale of any property condemned, forfeited, or subject to judicial foreclosure in federal cases. Marshals administer the Department of Justice's Asset Forfeiture Program, managing and disposing of homes, cars, boats, and other property seized from criminal defendants by U.S. attorneys or other federal law enforcement agencies under the Comprehensive Crime Control Act of 1984. Congress passed that law to punish drug dealers, members of organized crime syndicates, and other wealthy offenders by stripping them of cash and any property acquired through criminal activity. Under provisions of an Equitable Sharing Program, state and local police may share in the proceeds of criminal property seized within their jurisdictions.

Although it maintains no prisons of its own, the U.S. Marshals Service is also responsible for supervising and transporting federal prisoners before, during, and after trials (unless they are acquitted). That duty includes finding space for detainees in local jails, providing all necessary medical care, and housing material witnesses or the children of federal prisoners when no other relatives are able to do so. In 1995 the Marshals Service joined forces with the U.S. Bureau of Immigration and Customs Enforcement to create the Justice Prisoner and Alien Transportation System, which receives more than 1,000 daily requests for shipment of prisoners between judicial districts, from one prison to another, and to or from foreign countries.[10]

WITNESS SECURITY

In 1970, influenced by 20 years of federal investigation and the fresh publicity surrounding the publication of author Mario Puzo's best-selling 1969 Mafia novel, *The Godfather,* Congress passed the Organized Crime Control Act. That law provided the first legal definition of organized crime—also called "racketeering"—and increased penalties for specific crimes commonly associated with gangsters.

The new law also recognized that Mob-related crimes often go unpunished because crucial witnesses are threatened, terrorized, and even killed before they have a chance to testify in court. To solve that problem, Title V of the Organized Crime Control Act created the federal Witness Security Program (WITSEC) and handed responsibility for its administration to the U.S. Marshals Service.

WITSEC guards witnesses and members of their families by relocating them and furnishing new lives, complete with different names, false employment and school records, drivers' licenses, and Social Security numbers—anything, in short, to throw potential assassins off the scent and keep the witnesses alive.

In cases where a threat persists, as when a witness testifies against members of a surviving criminal gang, protection may extend for the rest of a witness's life. Various rules prevent contact with any relatives or former friends outside the WITSEC program, and since protected witnesses are sometimes "former" criminals themselves, violation of a strict ban on any illegal behavior may result in expulsion from the program.

Since 1971 the Marshals Service has relocated more than 8,200 federal witnesses and 9,800 family members. Service spokespersons report that no protected individual who followed WITSEC's rules has ever been unmasked and harmed, but 17 percent of those enrolled revert to criminal behavior and wind up in jail.[11] In April 2009 WITSEC was embarrassed by the conviction of a deputy marshal who sold WITSEC information to members of the Chicago Mafia, but no murders resulted from those leaks.

FUGITIVE INVESTIGATIONS

The Marshals Service leads all other federal law enforcement agencies in the pursuit and capture of fugitives from justice. In any given year, 55 percent of all arrested federal fugitives are caught by U.S. marshals—more than 36,600 federal offenders were jailed in 2008 alone. During the same year, marshals worked with other agencies to arrest more than 73,000 state and local fugitives, clearing a total of 90,600 felony warrants.[12]

U.S. marshals use a variety of methods to apprehend fugitives. In 1983 the service established its 15 Most Wanted Fugitive Program, patterned on the FBI's Ten Most Wanted list created in 1950. Candidates for the 15 Most Wanted roster are criminals with histories of violence and offenders whose latest crimes pose a significant threat to public safety. Recent additions to the list include murderers, sexual predators,

A U.S. marshal holds a "Most Wanted" flyer depicting a man on the 15 Most Wanted Fugitive list in June 2008. The fugitive, Elliott Evans Stamps, was eventually apprehended. *(Hulton-Deutsch Collection/Corbis)*

drug kingpins, and fugitive members of organized crime. Aside from traditional "Wanted" posters circulated to law enforcement agencies and U.S. post offices, members of the Top 15 dishonor roll are also profiled on the Marshals Service Web site at http://www.usmarshals.gov/investigations/most_wanted.

Marshals do not wait idly for local officers or private citizens to locate fugitives at large. In 1985 the service established a Major Case Fugitive Program to actively pursue fugitives who threaten public safety. The Marshals Service also serves as the lead agency in 91 interagency fugitive task forces, which include members drawn from other federal, state, and local law enforcement agencies.[13] Furthermore, the Marshals Service also has exclusive statutory responsibility for all international extraditions of prisoners to the United States, whatever the charges or jurisdiction involved.

(Continues on page 20)

"SHADOW STALKERS"

Toronto's police department created the first recognized special response team in 1965. The Los Angeles Police Department (LAPD) coined the famous "SWAT" name two years later and often claims credit for starting the trend in paramilitary policing. Four years after the LAPD first made headlines with the SWAT concept, in April 1971, the Marshals Service created the first federal SWAT team, dubbed the Special Operations Group (SOG). The FBI rushed to catch up with regional SWAT teams, but did not create its specialized Hostage Rescue Team until 1982.[14]

The SOG's mission statement describes it as "a specially trained and highly disciplined tactical unit. It is a self-supporting response team capable of responding to emergencies anywhere in the United States or its territories."[15] It maintains a small cadre of officers on full-time alert at the Marshals Service Tactical Operations Center at Camp Beauregard, Louisiana, prepared to fly out at a moment's notice, but the majority of SOG members are deputy marshals assigned to normal duties nationwide, remaining on call 24 hours per day for emergency missions.

Emergency missions include the full range of duties assigned to any SWAT team—apprehending armed fugitives, defusing hostage situations, protecting dignitaries, and serving high-risk warrants—plus tasks unique to the Marshals Service: transporting dangerous federal prisoners, providing witness security, seizing criminal assets, and securing federal courts against attack or sabotage. SOG's best-known missions during the past three decades include the following:

- SOG was deployed to maintain security during the American Indian Movement's (AIM) occupation of Wounded Knee, on South Dakota's Pine Ridge Sioux Reservation, between February 27 and May 5, 1973. During that siege, two AIM members were killed and Deputy Marshal Lloyd Grimm was paralyzed from the waist down by a gunshot wound to the spine.

- In November 1987 Cuban detainees facing deportation seized control of the federal prison in Atlanta, Georgia, capturing 75 hostages. SOG marshals and U.S. Army Special Forces troops surrounded the prison for an 11-day siege before negotiators secured release of the hostages.[16]
- On January 3, 1990, following the arrest of Panamanian dictator Manuel Noriega on drug-trafficking charges, SOG marshals escorted him to the United States for trial. In 1992 Noriega received a 40-year sentence, later reduced to 30 years on appeal.
- In August 1992 SOG officers tried to arrest Randall Weaver, a neo-Nazi hermit charged with federal firearms violations in Idaho. Weaver's son killed Deputy Marshal William

(continues)

Heavily armed members of the U.S. Marshal Special Operations Group arrive at a courthouse to provide security for the ongoing hearings for suspected terrorists. *(J.P. Moczulski/AFP/Getty Images)*

(continued)

Degan and was slain by other marshals, prompting a controversial 10-day siege. SOG headquarters in Louisiana is named in Marshal Degan's honor.

At last report, SOG consisted of four primary teams with 12 members each, plus 14 members on constant alert at Camp Beauregard. Service spokesmen report that 10 percent of SOG's members are female marshals, all of whom successfully completed the same rigorous training in marksmanship, close-quarters battle techniques, helicopter insertion, and other tactical exercises as their male counterparts. SOG training spans four weeks, with 15 to 17 hours per day consumed by physical training and classroom instruction.[17]

(Continued from page 17)

Since 2005 the Marshals Service, cooperating with more than 1,400 other law enforcement agencies across the United States, has conducted a series of fugitive roundups under the code name Operation FALCON (*F*ederal *a*nd *L*ocal *C*ops *O*rganized *N*ationally). By 2010 those sweeps had resulted in 91,086 arrests and 117,874 warrants cleared.[18]

HOMELAND SECURITY

The Marshals Service is not governed directly by the U.S. Department of Homeland Security, created in November 2002, but it does participate in America's war on terrorism, which launched after the tragic airline hijackings of September 11, 2001. Its Investigative Operations Division contributes to that global campaign with programs that include

- the International Investigations Branch, which conducted 857 deportations and extraditions, to and from 60 foreign countries, in the year 2008 alone.[19] Any terrorist suspects captured abroad and extradited for trial on American soil are transported by U.S. marshals.

- operation of foreign field offices in Mexico, Jamaica, and the Dominican Republic, coupled with coordination of law enforcement programs along the U.S. borders with Canada and Mexico.
- tactical and strategic intelligence support provided to other agencies by the Marshals Service's Air Surveillance Branch, Criminal Investigation Branch, and Electronic Surveillance Branch.
- the Explosive Detection Canine Program with eight teams in service nationwide, providing security for National Security Special Events which include presidential inaugurations, Democratic and Republican Party National Conventions, and various sporting events such as the Olympic Games, the Super Bowl, and the World Series.
- the Continuity of Operations Plan designed to ensure that essential government functions continue despite a wide range of potential emergencies. This plan includes maintenance of an Emergency Operations Center activated at times of national crisis or during catastrophic events.
- the Special Operations Group, created in 1971, which ranks as one of the first federal Special Weapons and Tactics (SWAT) teams, consisting of handpicked deputy U.S. marshals.

Early Marshals

Augusta, Georgia

U.S. Marshal Robert Forsyth expected trouble on January 11, 1794. His assignment that day was routine—delivering court papers for a civil lawsuit—but the defendants, brothers Beverly and William Allen, had a history of trouble with the law, so Forsyth took two deputies with him.

The Allens had been ducking service of the summons, but a local resident had reported their location to Marshal Forsyth. Arriving at the house, Forsyth and his deputies found the Allens talking to friends. Hoping to spare the brothers from embarrassment, Forsyth asked them to speak with him privately. Instead, the Allens ran into the house, rushed upstairs, and locked themselves in a bedroom.

Marshal Forsyth and his deputies followed the brothers and tried to enter the room. Beverly Allen fired a pistol through the door, striking Forsyth in the head and killing him instantly. Before Allen could reload his single-shot weapon, Forsyth's deputies arrested him and hauled him off to jail—but he would not stand trial. Soon after his arrest, Allen escaped from custody and fled the state. He was traced to Kentucky, but the U.S. marshal there had no authority to hold him for a crime committed in Georgia. Allen remained in Kentucky and died there in 1817. Robert Forsyth was the first of 235 U.S. marshals killed in the line of duty.[1]

SECURING JUSTICE

The U.S. Constitution established the U.S. federal government in June 1788, but much work remained to be done when Congress met for the first time in March 1789. One of its first duties was the creation of a federal court system, vaguely described in the Constitution as consisting of "one supreme Court, and . . . such inferior Courts as the Congress may from time to time ordain and establish."[2]

The result of that effort was the Judiciary Act of 1789, passed on September 24, which fixed the number of Supreme Court justices at six (later increased to nine) and created 13 judicial districts within the 11 states that had ratified the Constitution (later joined by North Carolina and Rhode Island in 1790). Finally, the law created the office of Attorney General and decreed that each judicial district should have one U.S. attorney and one U.S. marshal, who was empowered to choose deputies.[3]

President George Washington chose Virginia Governor Edmond Randolph as the first attorney general, and wrote to Randolph on September 28, 1789, saying:

> Impressed with a conviction that the due administration of justice is the firmest pillar of good Government, I have considered the first arrangement of the Judicial department as essential to the happiness of our Country, and to the stability of its political system; hence the selection of the fittest characters to expound the laws, and dispense justice, has been an invariable object of my anxious concern.[4]

Washington's concern extended beyond the choice of qualified judges to the selection of U.S. marshals. In fact, the president had chosen 13 candidates by September 26, two days after Congress passed the Judiciary Act.[5]

FIRST TO SERVE

Washington's choices set the standard for U.S. marshals to follow. All were prominent, politically active men in their states, and most were veterans of the Revolutionary War. Most also supported the Federalist Party. The original baker's dozen included the following individuals:

- *Clement Biddle* (1740–1814) was the first marshal of Pennsylvania and a partner in his family's Philadelphia shipping company until the war with England ruined it. In 1775 he organized a company of Philadelphia volunteers, and in July 1776 was appointed to serve as deputy quartermaster-general for the Pennsylvania and New York militias. He fought in the battles of Trenton, Brandywine, Germantown, and Monmouth, spending the cruel winter of 1777–78 with George Washington's troops at Valley Forge. At war's end, Biddle served as a marshal of the Admiralty Courts, which preceded establishment of federal courts under the Constitution. He resigned as Pennsylvania's marshal at the end of his first term, but later joined the state militia to suppress the Whiskey Rebellion of 1794.
- *Phillip Bradley* (1738–1821) was elected to Connecticut's General Assembly in 1769 and held that post until 1791, interrupted during the Revolutionary War by service in the Continental army. During the war, he performed special assignments for General Washington, including pursuit of deserters and investigation of misconduct among army officers. Bradley served as a marshal until 1802, doubling as a justice of the peace from 1793 to 1801.
- *Edward Carrington* (1748–1810) was a Virginia lawyer, politician, and personal friend of George Washington. He advised America's first president on selection of appointed officeholders. As an officer in the Revolutionary War, he saw action at Hobkirk's Hill and Yorktown. Carrington spent two years as Virginia's U.S. marshal, and then transferred to supervise liquor production within his home state. He served as jury foreman at Aaron Burr's treason trial in 1807, and was twice elected mayor of Richmond, Virginia, between 1807 and 1810.
- *Henry Dearborn* (1751–1829) studied medicine before the Revolutionary War, but never practiced. After the war, he settled in Maine and served in its militia, rising to the rank of major general before Washington chose him as the district's first U.S. marshal. In that post, he performed the first federal execution, hanging murderer Thomas Bird in June 1790. Dearborn ended his career as a marshal upon his election to Congress in 1793, and held that seat until 1797.

He returned to military service in the War of 1812, but his failed invasion of Canada forced his retirement in July 1813. President James Madison nominated Dearborn as secretary of war, but public protests defeated that effort.

- *Robert Forsyth* (1754–94), first U.S. marshal of Georgia, did not arrive in that state until 1785. By 1792 he was a prosperous farmer and justice of the peace. Forsyth was starting his fifth year as marshal when he was murdered by Beverly Allen. His son, John Jr., later served as Georgia's governor.
- *Isaac Huger* (1742–97) was the son of a wealthy South Carolina planter. He fought hostile Cherokees at age 18 and represented his state in the Continental Congress 15 years later. Serving as a colonel in the Revolutionary War, he was wounded at the Battle of Stono Ferry, but recovered in time to fight at Savannah and Hobkirk's Hill. Elected to South Carolina's state legislature in 1782, Huger held that post until President Washington chose him as the state's first U.S. marshal. Declining health forced his retirement in August 1793.
- *Jonathan Jackson* (1743–1810), first marshal of Massachusetts, prospered in business and entered politics in 1775. Although he did not serve in the Revolutionary War, his companies furnished supplies to the Continental army. Critics in the Continental Congress accused Jackson of marking up his prices 2,000 percent, but he denied the charge and finished the war nearly bankrupt from personal loans to the new American government. He led troops during Shays' Rebellion in 1787, and won election to the state senate in 1789. He left the Marshals Service to become a revenue inspector in 1791, later serving as state treasurer and as first president of the Boston Bank.
- *Thomas Lowry* (1737–1806) was born in Ireland and immigrated to New Jersey with his family at age 10. He served in the First Continental Congress, and then joined New Jersey's militia during the Revolutionary War. A personal friend of George Washington, Lowry served as New Jersey's first marshal until 1801, combining that duty with service in the state legislature.
- *Samuel McDowell Jr.* (1764–1834) ran away from his Virginia home at 17 to join the Continental army, arriving in time to fight in the Revolutionary War's last battle, at Yorktown. He moved to

Kentucky in 1784, continuing in military service in the Northwest Indian War. Kentucky was not yet a state when President Washington chose McDowell to serve as the region's first U.S. marshal. McDowell served three terms, hiring several of his relatives and in-laws as deputies.

- *Allan McLane* (1746–1825) was born in Pennsylvania and moved to Delaware at age 28. A hero of the Revolutionary War and noted for battlefield bravery, he also turned a profit by selling "beef" from British horses killed in combat to the Continental army. McLane resisted appointment as Delaware's first marshal, seeking a more lucrative post, but accepted the position at President Washington's request. In 1794 he complained to Washington that his post was "an office of considerable trust, but not profit."[6] Still, he remained as marshal until 1797, when he was promoted to collector of the Port of Wilmington, a job he held until his death.
- *John Parker* (1732–91) brought rare law enforcement experience to his post as New Hampshire's first U.S. marshal, having served as Rockingham County's sheriff since 1771. During his youth, he went to sea as a ship's master, later returning to New Hampshire as a merchant and insurance broker. He served two years as marshal before his death, at age 58.
- *Nathaniel Ramsay* (1741–1817) left Pennsylvania for Maryland in 1767. He prospered as an attorney, before the Revolutionary War sidetracked him into service with the Continental army. President Washington's appointment of Ramsay as Maryland's first U.S. marshal was, at least in part, a reward for his wartime service. He retained that post until 1794, when he became a naval officer in Baltimore; he served in that office until his death at age 76.
- *William Smith* (1755–1816), first U.S. marshal of New York, was an attorney who left his practice to serve as an officer of the Continental army. In 1785 he joined minister John Adams as secretary to the American legation in London, remaining overseas until 1788. Since New York City was the nation's capital until September 1791, Marshal Smith had frequent contact with President Washington. Smith left the Marshals Service after one year to become supervisor of revenue; later, he became surveyor for the Port of New York. He retired from public service when Thomas Jefferson became president in 1801.

NEW STATES, NEW MARSHALS

Five more states joined the Union during George Washington's presidency. Kentucky, admitted in June 1792, already had its U.S. marshal. The other new additions—North Carolina, Rhode Island, Vermont, and Tennessee—all needed officers to serve their federal courts.

John Skinner (1760–1819), a state legislator from 1784 to 1787 and a member of the Governor's Council in 1788–89, was North Carolina's first marshal. The governor described Skinner as a "gentleman of respectable connections and property," which included 850 acres of tobacco and 38 slaves.[7] He left the Marshals Service in 1794 to become North Carolina's commissioner of loans.

William Peck (1755–1832), the longest-serving original U.S. marshal, filled the post in Rhode Island from May 1790 until his retirement in 1810. Prior to his appointment, he served in the Continental army, then pursued a business career that left him penniless and out of work by 1790. After leaving the Marshals Service, he fell on hard times once again, saved from poverty by a congressional grant of pensions to Revolutionary War veterans in 1818.

Lewis Morris (1760–1825) served in the Revolutionary War, then as an aide to Robert Livingston, secretary of foreign affairs under the Articles of Confederation from 1781 to 1783. Morris moved to Vermont in 1786, achieving prominence in politics and commerce. Appointed as U.S. marshal in March 1791, he served until 1794, and then returned to active politics. He served six terms in the state legislature between 1795 and 1808, as well as three terms in Congress.

Robert Hays (1758–1819), a personal friend of war hero and future president Andrew Jackson (1767–1845), was captured by British troops during the American Revolution and spent a year as a prisoner of war. He served as a justice of the peace before filling the post as Tennessee's first U.S. marshal from 1796 to 1803.

WILD FRONTIER

As the United States expanded westward, new states and judicial districts required U.S. marshals. Some of the frontier's most famous—and controversial—lawmen wore a federal badge during the taming of the West. Aside from the renowned Earp brothers, the list of those marshals includes the following individuals:

- *James Butler "Wild Bill" Hickok* (1837–76) was a legendary gambler, gunfighter, and lawman. He killed at least seven men—including one of his own deputies, whom he shot accidentally in 1871.[8] Hickok entered law enforcement as a Kansas constable in 1857, and later served as a deputy U.S. marshal in Kansas from 1865 to 1867.

WYATT EARP (1848–1929)

The most famous of six brothers, Wyatt Earp was born in Illinois, but his family moved frequently—back and forth from Illinois to Iowa, then California, and finally settling in Lamar, Missouri, where his father served as constable. Earp held the same post in 1869, his first job in law enforcement. He married in January 1870, but his wife died before year's end. In May 1871 Earp was indicted for stealing license fees collected to support a local school. He fled town on a stolen horse and began to roam the West.[9]

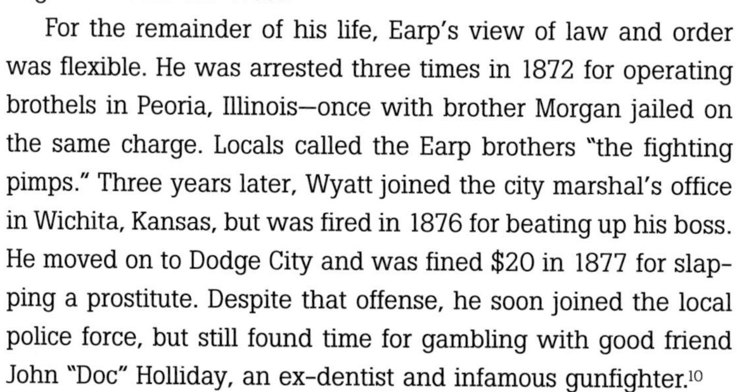

For the remainder of his life, Earp's view of law and order was flexible. He was arrested three times in 1872 for operating brothels in Peoria, Illinois—once with brother Morgan jailed on the same charge. Locals called the Earp brothers "the fighting pimps." Three years later, Wyatt joined the city marshal's office in Wichita, Kansas, but was fired in 1876 for beating up his boss. He moved on to Dodge City and was fined $20 in 1877 for slapping a prostitute. Despite that offense, he soon joined the local police force, but still found time for gambling with good friend John "Doc" Holliday, an ex-dentist and infamous gunfighter.[10]

The Earp brothers moved to Tombstone, Arizona, in 1879. James Earp ran a saloon, while brother Virgil was a deputy U.S. marshal and Wyatt rode shotgun on Wells Fargo stagecoaches. Trouble with a local band of outlaws called "the Cowboys" began in July 1880, when Virgil Earp accused one member of stealing army mules. By that time, Wyatt was a deputy sheriff for Pima County, serving under Sheriff John Behan, who became his mortal enemy. Wyatt quit that job in

Enemy Jack McCall killed Hickok during a poker game in Deadwood, Dakota Territory, in August 1876.

- *Patrick Garrett* (1850–1908) was both a deputy U.S. marshal and sheriff of Lincoln County, New Mexico, when he killed notorious outlaw Henry McCarty—alias "Billy the Kid"—in 1881.

November 1880 to support Behan's opponent in the next election. On the side, Wyatt ran a saloon and casino.

Tension escalated between the Earp brothers and the Cowboys until October 26, 1881, when the rivals met for a famous gunfight near Tombstone's O.K. Corral. Doc Holliday joined the Earps for that showdown, which left three Cowboys dead. The Earps were charged with murder, but a friendly judge dismissed the case. Unknown gunmen wounded Virgil Earp on December 28, whereupon U.S. Marshal Crawley Dake made Wyatt a deputy marshal (on a temporary basis), empowered to deputize others. When a sniper killed Morgan Earp on March 18, 1882, Wyatt naturally blamed the Cowboys.

Over the next three weeks, Wyatt, Warren Earp, Doc Holliday, and other deputies engaged in a "vendetta ride" against the Cowboys, killing at least four men (some reports list six). The posse then disbanded, and the Earps left Arizona. Wyatt returned to Dodge City in 1883, joining Bat Masterson and other gambler-gunfighters to form the Dodge City Peace Commission—a group that drove competitors out of business with threats and intimidation.[11]

Dime novels and exaggerated newspaper reports inflated Wyatt's life into a Western myth by the time he died in Los Angeles, in January 1929. A television series, *The Life and Legend of Wyatt Earp,* fictionalized his adventures from 1955 to 1961, and various films depicting Earp's exploits include *My Darling Clementine* (1946), *Gunfight at the O.K. Corral* (1957), *"Doc"* (1971), *Tombstone* (1993), *Wyatt Earp* (1994), and *Wyatt Earp: Return to Tombstone* (1994).

U.S. marshals—members of the Dodge City peace commission of 1882—appointed to bring law and order to the Western town are seen in this photo. Among those pictured are "Bat" Masterson *(top right)* and Wyatt Earp *(front row, second from left)*. *(AP Photo, File)*

- *William "Bat" Masterson* (1853–1921) was an overrated gunfighter who donned a deputy marshal's badge only after leaving the West for New York, in 1902.
- *Frank Dalton's* (1858–87) outlaw brothers formed the infamous Dalton Gang. Frank avoided his siblings and was killed from ambush by an Arkansas horse thief.
- *Elfego Baca* (1865–1945), sheriff of Socorro County, New Mexico, became a deputy U.S. marshal while studying law, later emerging as a prominent political figure.

ORRIN PORTER ROCKWELL (1813–78)

Orrin Rockwell was another colorful deputy marshal whose activities spanned both sides of the law. Although kind and generous to strangers, he was also a deadly gunman who once told Vice President Schuyler Colfax, "I never killed anyone who didn't need killing."[12] Unlike Wyatt Earp, however, Rockwell's crimes were committed in the name of religion.

A Massachusetts native, Rockwell joined the Mormon church in New York at age 20. By 1841 he was a bodyguard

(continues)

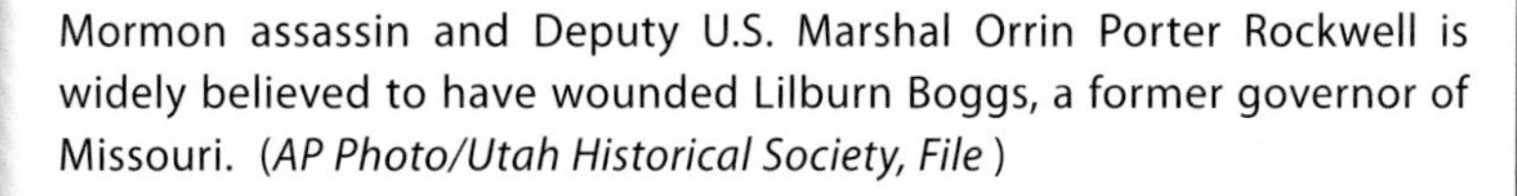

Mormon assassin and Deputy U.S. Marshal Orrin Porter Rockwell is widely believed to have wounded Lilburn Boggs, a former governor of Missouri. *(AP Photo/Utah Historical Society, File)*

(continued)

for church founder Joseph Smith Jr., but he failed to save Smith from an Illinois lynch mob in 1844. Rockwell was suspected in the 1842 Missouri shooting of dissident Mormon (and former Missouri governor) Lilburn Boggs, but he escaped prosecution by fleeing the state.[13] After Smith's murder, Rockwell served as a bodyguard for successor Brigham Young and joined the Mormon migration to present-day Utah. His activities there were even more controversial, as he became a leader of the Danites—a group of militant Mormons described as "avenging angels." In that role, Rockwell—nicknamed the "Destroying Angel"—traveled far and wide, killing dozens of persons who opposed the church or criticized it from within.[14]

During that same period, Rockwell served as a deputy U.S. marshal in Utah Territory, which was created by Congress in 1850. His service to the federal government was complicated by the Utah War of 1857–58, when officials in Washington, D.C., demanded that Mormons give up the practice of polygamy. Governor Brigham Young refused, prompting President James Buchanan to declare that Utah was in a state of rebellion against the United States. Violence followed—including the Mountain Meadows massacre, which claimed the lives of more than 100 travelers in September 1857—and Rockwell led raids to harass U.S. troops. Young finally surrendered in April 1858, ceding his office to Governor Alfred Cumming.

Those events ended Rockwell's service as a deputy U.S. marshal, but he remained active in the Mormon church for another 20 years. He died of natural causes in Salt Lake City on June 9, 1878. Rockwell's obituary, in the *Salt Lake Tribune,* stated that he had participated in at least 100 murders.[15]

- *John "Wolf Catcher" Abernathy* (1876–1941) was a deputy marshal in the Oklahoma Territory. He was best known for catching wolves bare-handed by forcing his fist down their throats.

Counterfeiting

Chesterfield, New Hampshire

Chesterfield is a small New England town. In the 2000 census it claimed 1,366 households and 3,542 residents.[1] On May 11, 2009, a well-dressed man wearing a gold badge and a pistol on his belt entered Chesterfield's Khyber Convenience Store. He identified himself as a U.S. marshal and told the store's owner that he was investigating a case of counterfeit money. The stranger examined $20 and $100 bills from the store's cash register, declared them counterfeit, and confiscated them.

He left in a new Jeep Grand Cherokee with official-looking license plates, and then drove on to the Big Deal Convenience Store, where the process was repeated. More money disappeared into the marshal's pocket, and he was gone.

Unfortunately, as police later confirmed, the "marshal" was a scam artist. Photos of the thief, taken by store surveillance cameras, identified him as 45-year-old John Baldasaro, a fugitive already charged with robbery, kidnapping, auto theft, and impersonating a police officer. Those crimes occurred in April 2009, when Baldasaro posed as a restaurant owner trying to sell a car; he then drove several different victims across state lines before stealing their money at gunpoint. The Jeep he drove on May 11 had been stolen in Maine.

Real members of the U.S. Marshals Fugitive Task Force captured Baldasaro on May 14, 2009, at a hotel in New York City. A deputy

(Continues on page 36)

CYBER-AGE COUNTERFEITERS

Currency is not the only thing subject to counterfeiting. During the past 25 years, criminals have made billions of dollars by selling counterfeit designer clothing, music and video recordings, computer games and software, and even vital hardware for computers and military vehicles or aircraft. Although U.S. marshals no longer track printers of counterfeit money, they are involved with other federal investigations of counterfeit merchandise.

A case in point occurred in January 2002, when marshals seized large quantities of counterfeit Compaq computer parts from the headquarters of Hardware 4 Less, a wholesaler in Bow, New Hampshire. Alerted by a customer's call for technical service on a fraudulent warranty, Compaq executives tipped U.S. marshals to the bootleg operation, which included production of counterfeit hard drives, memory boards, Compaq labels, software licenses, warranty booklets, and packing materials. Compaq spokesperson Elizabeth Gillan told reporters, "We will be seeking a permanent injunction and several million dollars in damages."[2]

While that lawsuit proceeded, federal prosecutors filed criminal charges against Mark Brunelle and David Ward, co-owners of Hardware 4 Less, on December 7, 2005. Both stood accused of selling counterfeit memory kits valued at $380,000 to vendors employed by two U.S. Department of Energy nuclear power plants located in New York and Pennsylvania. While the bootleg hardware was never installed, the multiple felony counts still carried a maximum penalty of 10 years in prison and a $2 million fine. Mark Brunelle negotiated a deal with authorities in the summer of 2006, pleading guilty on a single charge and receiving a sentence of 10 months' home confinement. David Ward pled guilty in April 2007, but the delay proved more costly: he received a four-month prison term.[3]

Hardware 4 Less was not the first bootleg computer operation broken up by U.S. marshals. In October 1992 marshals raided 10 sites owned by U-TOP Printing in California and New Jersey, seizing more than 150,000 counterfeit copies of Microsoft MS-DOS 5.0 valued at $9 million. The raiders filled 16 moving vans with confiscated software, manufacturing equipment, manuals, diskettes, holograms, and packaging supplies. In August 1996 Microsoft won $24.8 million dollars in civil damages. One month later, prosecutors indicted U-TOP owners James and Shirley Sung, along with three employees, on software piracy charges.[4]

In 1998 a private watchdog agency, the Business Software Alliance (BSA)—whose members include Adobe, Apple, Microsoft, Symantec, and other manufacturers—began collaborating with U.S. marshals to conduct surprise inspections at offices and homes suspected of using bootleg software. By 2003 the BSA had collected more than $37 million from various American companies caught using counterfeit products. One target, DuraSwitch Industries of Phoenix, Arizona, paid the BSA $135,000 in December 2000.[5] Suspicions of counterfeiting may be reported to the BSA's anti-piracy hotline at 1-888 NO PIRACY.

On October 15, 2000, marshals raided six computer companies in California and Colorado, seizing more than 5,000 counterfeit Adaptec host bus adapters, bootleg software, and documentation valued in excess of $1 million. The raided firms include Amotec, Global Source Technology, GlobalNet Computer Components, Globe Cargo, Lexy Pacific Corporation, and Unisun Group.[6]

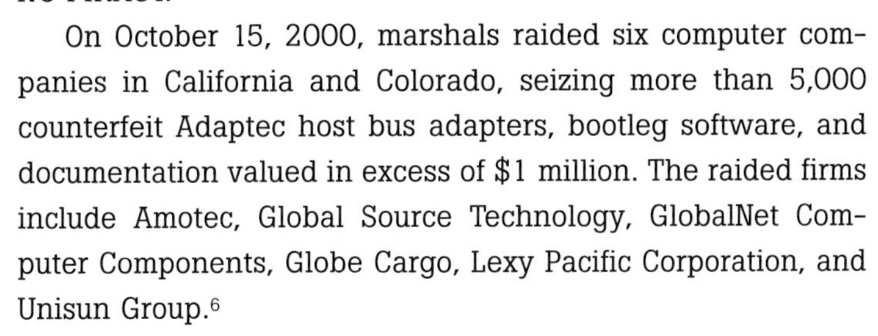

On April 21, 2002, local police joined U.S. Marshals to raid a fair at Grand Prairie, Texas, confiscating 1,681 bootleg CDs and 55 audiocassettes of music recorded by Latino artists including Vicente Fernandez, Enrique Iglesias, and Los Tigres del Norte. One vendor was charged with violating Texas's True Name and Address law, while another suspect escaped.[7]

(Continued from page 33)

marshal told reporters, "This was an attack on the reputation of the U.S. Marshals, and not something that is taken lightly; the quick and successful arrest of Baldasaro by the U.S. Marshals is evidence of that."[8] Baldasaro pled guilty to two felony-level counts of theft by deception and was sentenced to six to 12 years in New Hampshire State Prison.

BOOTLEG BUCKS

Counterfeit products include any imitation that violates a copyright or production monopoly held by a government or corporation. Counterfeit money is designed to resemble real currency and is produced and circulated as a form of fraud. On a small scale, counterfeit money cheats those who receive it in payment for goods or services. If widely circulated in large quantities, counterfeit currency may reduce the value of real money, cause inflation (higher prices), and destroy public confidence in national currency.

Counterfeiting has occurred since the invention of money. Early methods included the "clipping" or "shaving" of coins to reduce their weight, or mixing precious and base metals to produce facsimile coins of low value. British counterfeiters Thomas and Anne Rogers were sentenced to death by torture in 1690 for "Clipping 40 pieces of Silver"—a crime considered treason to the Crown.[9]

Modern counterfeiting normally involves paper currency, and in America its practice dates from the outbreak of the Revolutionary War.

COLONIAL CHAOS

America's economy was a shambles on the eve of revolution. Massachusetts printed the country's first paper money in 1690, soon followed by the other colonies. All were based on the English shilling, but each colony's money had a different value, ranging from five shillings per Georgia dollar to 32 and a half shillings per dollar in South Carolina. The Continental Congress made things worse in May 1775 when it ordered $2 million in new paper currency that included 11,800 $20 bills and 49,000 bills in each of eight more denominations, ranging from one to eight dollars.[10]

A warning against counterfeiting can be seen in the bottom right-hand corner of this ten schillings banknote of New York Colonial Currency issued in February 1771. *(Fotosearch/Getty Images)*

Printing currency with insufficient gold or silver to support it caused steep inflation. British troops compounded the problem with wagonloads of counterfeit Continental dollars, which they handed out free of charge to persons traveling through the rebellious colonies. As the war dragged on, the common phrase “not worth a Continental” indicated lack of public trust in American currency. Even legitimate money was nearly worthless, as it was backed by “anticipation” of tax revenue from the states that seldom reached Congress.[11] America won the war, but it nearly went bankrupt in the process.

RESTORING ORDER

The first U.S. government, under the Articles of Confederation and Perpetual Union (1781–88), still permitted each state to print its own currency, which was often rejected by neighboring states. Congress had no power to enforce laws or collect taxes, relying instead on requests for money, which states were free to refuse. Saddled with debts from

Starting in 1775, the Continental Congress introduced massive quantities of currency in various denominations, such as this six-dollar note, created in 1776. *(Getty Images)*

the war and unable to raise funds except by printing more currency, America's leaders watched the situation go from bad to worse.

The new U.S. Constitution, drafted in 1787 and ratified by nine of the 13 states in June 1788, addressed these problems directly. Article I, Section 8, declares that only Congress may "coin money [and] regulate the value thereof," and Section 10 drives home the point, forbidding any state from producing its own currency. In April 1792 Congress passed the Coinage Act, establishing the United States Mint and regulating the amount of gold and silver used in American coins. Curiously, however, local banks were still allowed to print their own paper money.[12]

That loophole encouraged counterfeiters to continue swindling the public and the government. Two of the most notorious practitioners in 18th-century America were Philip Alston and John Duff—both exiled from Kentucky in 1788 for counterfeiting—who later shared headquarters with Ohio River pirate Samuel Mason at Cave-in-Rock, Illinois. Residents of nearby Fort Massac hated Duff so much that they hired Shawnee tribesmen to kill him in June 1799. Alston's fate is unknown, but some reports claim that his outlaw son, Peter, was executed with frontier serial killer Wiley Harpe—another member of Mason's pirate crew—in 1804.

Four decades later, in April 1846, U.S. Marshal John McLean reported that a gang of counterfeiters was operating in Ohio. Because they received no payment for investigating federal crimes, and the Treasury Department refused to reimburse them, state officials refused to act. By winter 1847, Marshal McLean had identified "upwards of 50 counterfeiters in Ohio. Many of them [were] men of property and apparent respectability." He reported that fake currency was printed in "out of the way places: seldom in towns and cities. In brief, they practice their offenses in the most adroit manner. It is only by great skill, stratagem, and resolution that this class of men can be detected and brought to justice."[13]

In addition to the expense, chasing counterfeiters appeared to be a waste of time. Existing federal laws contained no penalties for possession of counterfeit money or printing equipment, or for selling fake bills as counterfeits. The only crime was passing off bogus money as real—

which generally led to the arrest of small-time counterfeiters operating on a local scale.

Marshal McLean received no support from Washington. Only in 1860, on the eve of civil war, did Congress finally create a $10,000 fund for investigation of counterfeiting—but even then, the secretary of the Treasury restricted funding to major cases. Marshal Walker's Ohio successor, Daniel Robertson, received five dollars per day to pursue "the most-secret and successful perpetrators of crime in the country."[14] Somehow, he rid Ohio of its major counterfeiters, chasing some into Kentucky and Virginia, but the national problem persisted.

SAMUEL CURTIS UPHAM (1819–85)

Samuel Upham was born in Vermont and left home at age 20, working as a clerk in New York before he joined the U.S. Navy, serving from 1842 to 1844. Next, he worked as a bookkeeper in Philadelphia, until the California gold rush drew him westward in 1849. After failing at mining, Upham started a newspaper in Sacramento, then sold it in 1850 and returned to Philadelphia. Over the next 11 years he wrote songs and newspaper articles and worked on a book about his California adventures.

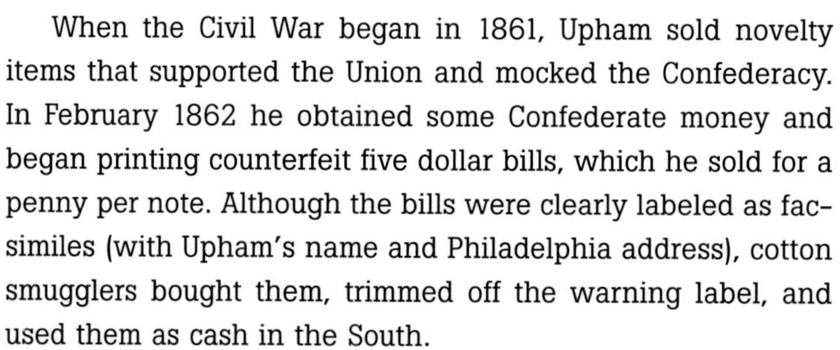

When the Civil War began in 1861, Upham sold novelty items that supported the Union and mocked the Confederacy. In February 1862 he obtained some Confederate money and began printing counterfeit five dollar bills, which he sold for a penny per note. Although the bills were clearly labeled as facsimiles (with Upham's name and Philadelphia address), cotton smugglers bought them, trimmed off the warning label, and used them as cash in the South.

As business boomed, Upham expanded his list of counterfeit Confederacy items. By May 1862 he was printing 12 different denominations of Confederate currency and postage stamps, selling the fake bills for five cents apiece. U.S. marshals investigated claims that he was also forging Union money, but they

And still, despite the Constitution and the Coinage Act of 1792, Congress limited its scrutiny of U.S. currency to gold and silver coins. In 1862 more than 1,000 banks nationwide printed their own paper currency. Counterfeiting flourished, with investigators estimating that one-third of all paper money in circulation was counterfeit.[15] This situation was especially dangerous as the United States plunged into a bloody civil war.

A HOUSE DIVIDED

War is often good for the economy because it stimulates industrial production and reduces unemployment. On the other hand, counterfeit

found no evidence and Secretary of War Edwin Stanton intervened to dismiss the case. Some authors claim that Stanton provided Upham with reams of paper used in standard currency to help him damage the Southern economy.[16]

Upham later claimed the he sold 1,564,000 counterfeit Confederate bills (with a face value of $15 million) between March 1862 and August 1863, and some historians believe that his fake bills totaled 3 percent of the South's total currency in circulation. When other counterfeiters followed his example, Upham cut his prices to outsell the competition. Rumors spread that Southern officials had offered a $10,000 reward for Upham delivered to Dixie dead or alive, and counterfeiters caught in the South were sentenced to death. Henry Foote, a member of the Confederate Congress, once claimed that Upham had done more to harm the South than Union General George McClellan's Army of the Potomac.[17]

At war's end, Upham abandoned counterfeiting to sell other novelties and hair dye—billed as "Best in the World"—while writing hymns on the side. Cancer claimed his life at age 66 in Philadelphia. Mystery surrounds the disposition of his fortune earned from counterfeiting, more than $50,000 of which is unaccounted for.[18]

money—whether produced by common criminals or a nation's enemies—may undermine a country's hopes for victory. Britain used "funny money" as a weapon in the Revolutionary War, and fake currency caused problems for both the Union and the Confederacy during the Civil War (1861–65).

In 1862, to fund its war effort, Congress passed the Legal Tender Act, which authorized the printing of $150 million in paper currency without the backing of precious metals. Those bills were nicknamed "greenbacks," for their color. This development encouraged counterfeiting in the North—and also in the South, where "Yankee" dollars were printed cheaply to flood the Union economy. At the same time, Philadelphia journalist Samuel Upham began printing fake Confederate money as a novelty item. Others soon did likewise, with criminal intent, perhaps encouraged by the U.S. government, inflicting serious damage on the South's economy.[19]

Passage of the National Bank Act in February 1863 raised more money for the Union war effort by encouraging Northern banks to buy federal bonds, while taxing state bonds out of existence. It also created an Office of the Comptroller of Currency within the Treasury Department, which was empowered to design paper money that would replace the different bills issued by various banks. When the first law failed to eliminate such banknotes, the National Bank Act of 1864—actually passed in March 1865—levied a 10 percent tax on such bills, forcing them out of circulation by 1866.

Meanwhile, counterfeiting was rampant on both sides of the Mason-Dixon Line. Approximately half of all the North's paper money was counterfeit by 1864. Historian Thomas Craughwell notes, "[l]ike the rest of the American public, counterfeiters adjusted to the new national currency quickly. In fact, they preferred it to the old banknotes. A Philadelphia shopkeeper who would have studied a fifty-dollar banknote from the Planter's Bank of Tennessee would accept a U.S. fifty-dollar bill without a second thought."[20] As the value of their own money declined, Confederate citizens also bought the fake Union currency.

While U.S. marshals tracked counterfeiters, state authorities generally did nothing. No major Northern city ever launched a campaign against counterfeiting during the Civil War, and rumors persist that highly placed U.S. officials encouraged the practice. Some historians claim that Secretary of War Edwin Stanton smuggled special paper from England, for use by Northern counterfeiters printing Confederate bills. Others say that William Wood, supervisor of Washington's Old Capitol Prison, sent counterfeit money to Union prisoners of war in Dixie, to buy clothes, food, and other items from their clueless jailers. That may explain why Secretary Stanton, seeking a director of anti-counterfeiting efforts in early 1865, chose Wood to lead the effort.[21]

Thus began the U.S. Secret Service, formally created on July 5, 1865. The Civil War had ended three months earlier, but counterfeiting continued. Within its first year of operation, the Secret Service arrested more than 200 counterfeiters and removed large amounts of bogus currency from circulation.[22] Even with the Secret Service hunting counterfeiters, though, U.S. marshals still pursued vendors of funny money on occasion. One such case cost a deputy marshal his life.

On May 11, 1877, brothers Dee and James Bailey spent the night at a hotel in Comanche, Texas. The next morning, before leaving town, they bought new clothes. The hotel manager, a Mr. Hill, soon discovered that the Baileys had paid for their lodging—and their clothing—with counterfeit coins. Hill reported the fraud to Maston Greene, deputy U.S. marshal for the Western District of Texas.

Deputy Marshal Greene pursued the suspects on horseback, taking Hill along to identify them. They overtook the Baileys 10 miles outside of town, commanding them to stop and surrender. Greene took Jim Bailey's pistol and a pocketful of counterfeit coins, but he overlooked Dee's rifle in a saddle boot. Dee Bailey drew the Winchester and ordered Greene to return the coins. Greene dropped them on the ground, then pulled his gun and fired at Dee Bailey, grazing his scalp. Bailey then shot Greene in the face and in the foot after Greene fell from his horse. The brothers fled, while Hill carried Deputy Greene to a nearby farmhouse. Greene died there at 7:30 P.M.

The Bailey brothers escaped and remained at large for six years, but Texans have long memories. Lawmen captured the brothers six years later, in 1883, and returned them to Comanche County for trial, but local residents were impatient. On September 19 a mob took the Baileys from jail and hanged them from a tree on the outskirts of town.[23]

Court Security

Topeka, Kansas

Jack Gary McKnight led a strange double life in America's heartland. Employed for 15 years by the Santa Fe Railroad, he spent most of that time in the company's accounting office, barely noticed by his coworkers. That changed in August 1992, when federal agents raided his home in Meriden, Kansas, seizing more than 100 marijuana plants, plus cultivation equipment and other drug paraphernalia, several weapons, and items of child pornography. McKnight's wife pled guilty on weapons charges, and he was convicted on multiple felony counts in Topeka's federal court, scheduled to return for sentencing on August 5, 1993.

At 8:30 that morning, McKnight blew up his truck outside the Jefferson County courthouse in Oskaloosa, and then drove another vehicle 23 miles to reach Topeka's Frank J. Carlson Federal Building. Armed with two pistols and several homemade pipe bombs, McKnight entered the building—which had no ground-floor security guards—and rode an elevator to the fourth floor, where federal trials are held.

Emerging from the elevator, McKnight met Court Security Officer Gene Goldsberry, a veteran of 35 years' service with the U.S. Marshals Service. His first shots killed Goldsberry and wounded a civilian bystander; others ran for their lives. McKnight then roamed the fourth floor, stopping a court clerk at one point and telling her, "You're not the one I'm looking for."[1] He fired shots through the courthouse windows at police gathered outside, and witnesses reported at least three explosions inside the building.

An hour passed before SWAT team officers found McKnight dead on the federal building's fourth floor, mangled by one of his own pipe bombs. Three other people were injured by shrapnel from the explosions, and a fourth hurt his back while crawling through a ceiling panel to escape. Authorities remain uncertain as to whether McKnight committed suicide or died in an accidental explosion.

SERVING THE COURTS

The same Judiciary Act of 1789 that established America's federal courts also ordered the appointment of U.S. marshals to serve those courts in various ways. Courthouse security—protection of judges, jurors, witnesses, and the physical courthouse itself—has always been an issue, and the modern age of terrorism makes that function of the U.S. Marshals Service even more important.

Today, those duties are performed by the service's Judicial Security Division (JSD), committed, in its own words, to "anticipating and deterring threats to the judiciary, and the continuous development and employment of innovative protective techniques."[2] The JSD is led by a deputy assistant director of the U.S. Marshals Service, who supervises both the Office of Protective Operations and the Office of Protective Intelligence, coordinating the activities of both departments within a program broadly termed Judicial Operations.

The Office of Protective Operations (OPO) consists of senior inspectors and program analysts who provide physical courthouse security, manage protective investigations, and conduct threat assessments for all levels of the federal judiciary, as well as the attorney general, various U.S. attorneys, and the director of the White House Office of National Drug Control Policy. On any given day, the OPO provides security for more than 2,000 federal judges and some 5,200 court employees throughout the United States and its territories. In the year 2009 alone, at least 1,300 threats against federal courts or court officers were analyzed and investigated by the OPO, with some cases resulting in 24-hour surveillance. During the same year, OPO agents coordinated 290 protective details aside from normal courthouse guard duties, furnished protective services to 163 judicial conferences or other critical meetings, and provided extraordinary security for 178 high-threat trials (including 96 terrorist cases).[3]

For much of its work, the OPO depends on information gathered by the Office of Protective Intelligence (OPI). The OPI staff includes senior inspectors, intelligence research specialists, and program analysts who coordinate information on threats or other security risks collected by local police, the FBI, Secret Service, and federal court officials. The OPI analyzes "inappropriate communications"—including verbal threats, phone calls, letters, and e-mails—to evaluate their risk potential, while providing round-the-clock responses through the relatively new Threat Management Center. Drawing on the expertise of instructors from the Marshals Service, FBI, Secret Service, U.S. Attorney's Office, Diplomatic Security Service, and ATF (Bureau of Alcohol, Tobacco, Firearms and Explosives), the OPI also trains deputy U.S. marshals and judicial security inspectors for courthouse security duties.

Judicial Services also includes various other programs, all of which are related to the safe and orderly conduct of federal courts. Funded by the Administrative Office of the United States Courts (AOUSC), they include the following:

- The *Office of Court Security* (OCS), including the Court Security Officer (CSO) Program, trains and deploys more than 4,800 CSOs to various federal courts. With an average 5,000 job applications per year, the OCS screens potential CSOs to ensure that specific background, physical, medical, and weapons qualifications standards are met. Before CSOs are assigned in the field, they undergo intensive training.
- The *Office of Security Contracts* (OSC) is responsible for acquisition of any and all security equipment, systems, and services from private contractors, including installation and maintenance; the office works with contract officer technical representatives in 94 judicial districts worldwide. Spending on the CSO Program alone tops $250 million per year for equipment and training. A second major area of responsibility involves contracts for security equipment at federal courthouses, which is installed by ADT Security Systems. Finally, the OSC also maintains an extensive Home Intru-

sion Detection System Program for federal judges, covering 1,650 private homes since December 2005.[4]

- The *Office of Security Systems* (OSS) is assigned to deploy and coordinate installation of electronic security devices at federal courthouses, including perimeter security, access control, closed-circuit TV, and alarm reporting systems. The OSS also designs "low-profile weapons-screening stations"—checkpoints manned by CSOs equipped with metal detectors and X-ray equipment—that "provide protection while blending into lobby architecture."[5]
- The *Office of Financial Management* (OFM) receives funds from the AOUSC and disburses them as needed to maintain courthouse security. In 2008 the OFM received $342.3 million, 88.6 percent of which was spent on CSO operations, while 9.4 percent was used for the purchase and maintenance of security equipment and 2 percent was spent on management and administration.[6] OFM expenses include staff salaries and payments due under contract to private security firms.

In 2007 the Judicial Security Division established the National Center for Judicial Security (NCJS), which, as described by the U.S. Marshals Service, "provides a wide range of services and support to federal, state, local, and international jurisdictions as they seek advice and assistance on questions of judicial security." Its tasks include creating "programs and activities directly related to threat assessment, training, information sharing, and technology review."[7]

SERVICE OF PROCESS

The judicial functions of the Marshals Service are not limited to courthouse security. Besides guarding judges, jurors, and witnesses, U.S. marshals serve as the enforcement arm of America's federal courts, required to execute any judicial order as directed. That duty includes service of process—the delivery of summons, injunctions, warrants, or writs issued by federal judges. The types of process served by members of the Marshals Service are criminal, civil, foreign, and admiralty.

Criminal process includes all documents and orders related to trial and punishment of federal crimes. Various forms include the following:

- *Criminal subpoenas* command the appearance of an individual or the production of specific items (often documents or records) before a federal judge. Criminal subpoenas may be served anywhere in the world, but service by a U.S. marshal is restricted to the United States or its territories.
- A *criminal summons,* delivered in lieu of arrest, requires a defendant's appearance in court at a given time and location.
- *Writs of habeas corpus* command that custodians of another person (usually jailers) deliver that individual for prosecution or to testify as a witness.
- *Removal warrants* order the removal of a prisoner from one judicial district to another for prosecution on outstanding charges.
- *Judgments and commitments* state the verdict in federal trials and the sentence imposed on convicted defendants, including the length of imprisonment.

Civil process includes 13 different orders related to civil lawsuits conducted in federal courts. They include the following:

- The *summons and complaint* informs a defendant of a plaintiff's accusations, instructing the defendant when and where to report for trial.
- *Subpoenas* require the appearance of witnesses, with or without specific pieces of evidence.
- A *juror summons* orders citizens to report for jury duty.
- A *writ of attachment* is an order to "attach" or seize an asset, per the judgment issued by the court. A prejudgment writ of attachment may be issued prior to legal proceedings in order to freeze the assets of a defendant during trial.
- *Writs of sequestration* deliver property to the Marshals Service for safekeeping prior to trial.
- *Writs of replevin* are pretrial orders commanding marshals to take custody of suspected stolen property.
- *Writs of assistance* demand delivery of a deed, document, or right of ownership.
- *Warrants of arrest in rem* enforce a maritime lien against a particular ship or cargo.

ADT SECURITY SERVICES

ADT Security Services began its long corporate life as American District Telegraph in 1874. Tyco International, a security firm with 6 million clients worldwide, bought the company in 1998, then purchased ADT's main rival—SecurityLink—in 2001. Today, based in Boca Raton, Florida, ADT provides a wide range of security services, including access control, alarm monitoring, fire protection, intrusion detection, medical alert system monitoring, and video surveillance through more than 180 sales and service offices nationwide.[8]

A major part of ADT's business involves collaboration with federal agencies to provide state-of-the-art security equipment and hands-on training in its proper use. Today, ADT is the exclusive supplier and installer of security equipment for the U.S. Marshals Service, covering more than 700 federal courthouses in the United States and its far-flung territories. ADT provides a full range of equipment that links federal courts and their judges' chambers to local U.S. attorney's offices, the General Service Administration, and the U.S. Department of Homeland Security's Federal Protective Service.[9] Equipment supplied and maintained by ADT includes

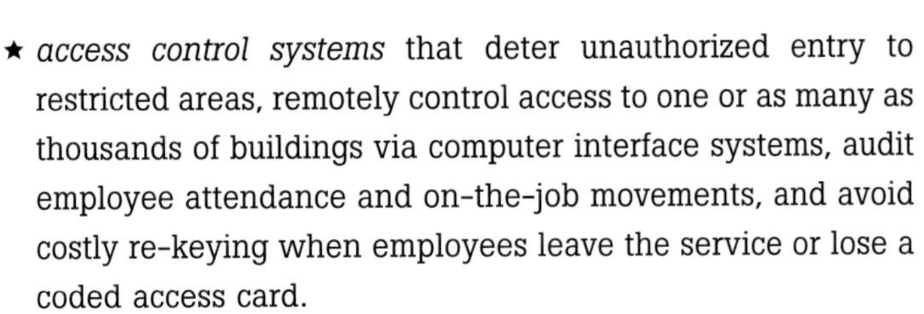

- *access control systems* that deter unauthorized entry to restricted areas, remotely control access to one or as many as thousands of buildings via computer interface systems, audit employee attendance and on-the-job movements, and avoid costly re-keying when employees leave the service or lose a coded access card.

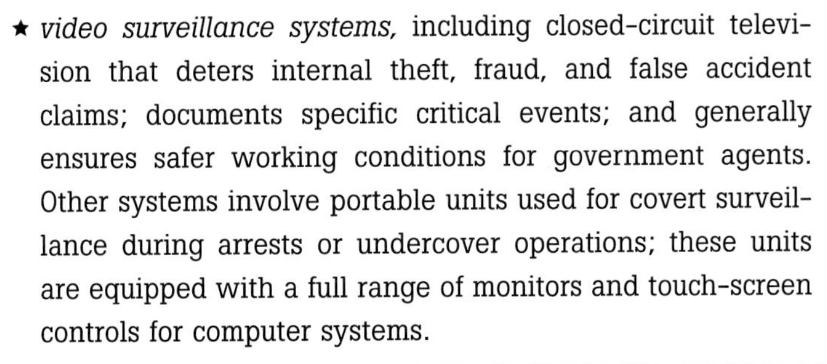

- *video surveillance systems,* including closed-circuit television that deters internal theft, fraud, and false accident claims; documents specific critical events; and generally ensures safer working conditions for government agents. Other systems involve portable units used for covert surveillance during arrests or undercover operations; these units are equipped with a full range of monitors and touch-screen controls for computer systems.

- *Writs of body attachment* command U.S. marshals to deliver persons found to be in civil contempt of court.
- *Injunctions* or *restraining orders* ban specified activities, either temporarily or permanently.
- *Writs of garnishment* seize a debtor's property held by third parties (such as a defendant's paycheck).
- *Writs of execution* order marshals to enforce a court's order for payment of money.
- *Notices of condemnation* are issued against property scheduled for sale by court order to satisfy monetary judgments or in cases of asset forfeiture.

Foreign process involves service of federal court orders in other countries. While the Marshals Service is legally responsible for that service, marshals generally are not permitted to conduct service on foreign soil. In most cases, foreign service is conducted by a designated private contractor, Process Forwarding International, based in Seattle, Washington.

Admiralty process involves the Marshals Service in cases of maritime liens or actions against specific persons. Federal courts may order marshals to arrest, attach, or garnish a ship, property, or cargo, and to hold it pending further order of the court.

PRISONER CUSTODY

As officers of the federal courts, U.S. marshals also take custody of prisoners arrested by any federal law enforcement agency, assuming responsibility for their housing and transportation between arrest and the time they are either acquitted at trial or delivered to the Federal Bureau of Prisons (FBP) for incarceration. Detainees who are denied bail or cannot afford it remain technically in custody of the Marshals Service, although they may be housed in local jails or FBP detention facilities. Responsibility for prisoners awaiting trial includes medical care and isolation of prisoners with contagious diseases. Marshals may also be responsible (when no other caretakers are available) for housing a prisoner's dependent children and procuring lodging for "alien material witnesses."[10]

"MAXIMUM JOHN"

John Howland Wood Jr. was born in Texas on March 31, 1916. He received a BA in business administration in 1935 from St. Mary's University in San Antonio. Three years later, he graduated from the University of Texas School of Law. He practiced law in San Antonio from 1938 to 1970, interrupted by service in the U.S. Navy during World War II. President Richard Nixon nominated Wood as a federal judge for the Western District of Texas in October 1970, and the U.S. Senate confirmed his appointment six weeks later.

As a judge, Wood earned the nickname "Maximum John" for his habit of sentencing convicted felons to the maximum prison terms allowed by law. One criminal who knew and feared Wood's reputation was Jamiel "Jimmy" Chagra, a major Texas drug trafficker arrested in 1978 on charges of smuggling marijuana into the United States from Mexico. Under federal law, based on the quantity of drugs involved, Chagra faced a life prison term if convicted in Judge Wood's courtroom. Rather than take that risk, he hired contract killer Charles Harrelson—father of actor Woody Harrelson—to murder Wood. Harrelson shot and killed Wood outside his home on May 29, 1979. Chagra went to trial before another judge, receiving a 30-year sentence.

An anonymous tip identified Harrelson as Wood's assassin, and federal agents confirmed it by recording a conversation between Chagra and his brother Joseph at Leavenworth federal prison. Harrelson received two life terms, one for Wood's murder and another for a killing committed in 1968. Jamiel Chagra was acquitted of murder, but his wife and his brother received prison terms for conspiracy. Chagra then admitted his participation in the crime, to free his wife from jail, but she died from cancer while in custody. Chagra was paroled in December 2003 and died (also from cancer) in July 2008. Charles Harrelson died in prison on March 15, 2007, of unspecified natural causes. San Antonio's federal building and a local high school are named in honor of Judge John Wood.

A suspected terrorist supporter is escorted to a prison van by a U.S. marshal after his court appearance. *(AP Photo/J. Pat Carter)*

The Marshals Service also retains custody of convicted federal defendants before they are delivered to FBP officials and during any transfer between prisons, to and from subsequent trials, to medical facilities outside of prison, and so on. In 1995 the Marshals Service and the Bureau of Immigration and Customs Enforcement (ICE) joined forces to create the Justice Prisoner and Alien Transportation System (JPATS) (managed by the Marshals Service) to securely transport prisoners and criminal aliens. On any given day, JPATS handles more than 1,000 requests to move prisoners between judicial districts, to and from prisons, or to and from foreign nations—an average of 300,000 prisoners moved each year.[11]

JPATS is presently the only government-operated, regularly scheduled passenger airline in the United States. It maintains a fleet of jet aircraft that transport prisoners and aliens at a fraction of the cost charged by commercial airlines. Military and civilian law enforcement agencies also use the service, under contract with the government. JPAT operates from headquarters in Kansas City, Missouri, serving 40 domestic and international cities. Air fleet operations are based in Oklahoma City, with hubs in Alexandria, Louisiana; Mesa, Arizona; and Aguadilla, Puerto Rico. Responsibility for ground transportation is shared by the Marshals Service, ICE, and the Federal Bureau of Prisons.[12]

ASSET FORFEITURE

Two federal statutes passed in 1970, the Racketeer Influenced and Corrupt Organizations (RICO) Act and the Controlled Substances Act, allow the U.S. government to seize money and property—including vehicles, homes, businesses, real estate, weapons, jewelry, and so on—derived from various illegal activities. These measures were enacted to prevent convicted criminals (often members of organized crime or large corporations) from leaving prison with their illicit fortunes still intact. In 1984 the Comprehensive Crime Control Act created the Department of Justice Assets Forfeiture Fund (AFF), which sells confiscated property and uses the money obtained to benefit law enforcement.

Under terms of the Comprehensive Crime Control Act, the U.S. Marshals Service is responsible for administration of the AFF. Marshals take custody of confiscated property and sell an average 8,400 items per year, raising some $97 million.[13] A national list of private contractors that handle asset forfeiture sales is available from the Marshals Service online at http://www.pueblo.gsa.gov/cic_text/fed_prog/selerlst/selerlst.htm.

Members of the federal "asset forfeiture community," receiving income from the sale of confiscated property, include the U.S. Marshals Service, the FBI, the DEA, the ATF, the Department of Homeland Security, and various U.S. attorneys' offices.[14] (A parallel forfeiture program, administered by the Treasury Department, handles property seized by the Criminal Investigation Division of the Internal Revenue Service.) The federal government also maintains the Equitable Sharing Program, created under terms of the Debt Collection Improvement Act of 1996, which shares proceeds from the sale of confiscated property with state and local police departments that participated in specific investigations.

Deputy U.S. Marshals and U.S. Postal Inspectors seize an automobile from the home of Shawn R. Merriman in Aurora, Colorado, in April 2009. The Department of Justice began seizing assets at the home and other property belonging to Merriman in connection with an investigation into a Ponzi scheme. *(AP Photo/ Ed Andrieski)*

Various states have followed Washington's example in seizing suspected criminal assets, with mixed results. In some states, police routinely confiscate large quantities of money found in the possession of suspected criminals, either on their persons or hidden in homes, vehicles, and so on. Oversight in such cases may be limited to local judges, and accusations of corruption or theft by police are common. For example, police in Tenaha, Texas, stopped 150 motorists between 2006 and 2008, seizing cash and other property valued in excess of $3 million. Most of those detained were African Americans or Latinos, and few were charged with any crimes. Exposure of that practice in the *Houston Chronicle* prompted Senator John Whitmire to say, "The idea that people lose their property but are never charged, and never get it back, that's theft as far as I'm concerned."[15]

Difficult Tasks

Boston, Massachusetts

Anthony Burns was 20 years old when he fled Virginia to escape slavery in 1854. He reached Boston safely, but slave catchers found him and placed him under arrest on May 24 of the same year. Although slavery was banned in Massachusetts, the Fugitive Slave Act of 1850 required U.S. marshals to help Southern slave owners recover their lost "property."

On May 26 Deputy Marshal James Batchelder reported for duty at Boston's courthouse, where Burns was confined. Outside, an angry mob of abolitionists had gathered, armed and anxious to release Burns. Their legal pleas had failed, so they turned to force.

Batchelder and his fellow deputies stood fast when rioters stormed the courthouse, smashing through its doors. Gunfire blazed in the lobby, followed by hand-to-hand fighting, before police and state militia arrived to disperse the mob. By then, Deputy Batchelder had suffered fatal wounds, becoming the second U.S. marshal killed on duty. Eighteen rioters were jailed—two charged with killing Batchelder—but no record of their trial survives today.[1]

Anthony Burns returned to Virginia, where his owner promptly sold him to another slave owner in North Carolina. Abolitionists later purchased his freedom, and Burns served as a non-ordained minister until his premature death at age 28, in 1862.

UNWELCOME DUTIES

All police officers perform tasks that make them unpopular with some citizens, and U.S. marshals are no exception. Their first thankless task came in 1791, when Congress sought to raise money by taxing whiskey. Secretary of the Treasury Alexander Hamilton supported the tax "more as a measure of social discipline than as a source of revenue," but also admitted that he "wanted the tax imposed to advance and secure the power of the new federal government."[2]

Whiskey distillers bitterly opposed the new law. Open rebellion flared in Pennsylvania during July 1794, overwhelming U.S. Marshal David Lenox and his deputies. Supreme Court Justice James Wilson said the rebels were "too powerful to be suppressed by the powers vested in the Marshal of that district," but Lenox rode with 12,950 state militiamen to face the insurgents on September 7.[3] The troops arrested 150 whiskey rebels by November, but only two—Judge Robert Philson and Quaker Herman Husband—were convicted of treason. President Washington pardoned both men. The whiskey tax remained in force until 1801.

Protesters tar and feather a tax collector during the Whiskey Rebellion in Pennsylvania in the 1790s. A group of marshals participated in the suppression of the uprising. *(North Wind Picture Archives via AP Images)*

SEDITION

In the summer of 1798 Congress passed four laws commonly labeled the Alien and Sedition Acts. One—the Naturalization Act, repealed in 1802—extended the mandatory residency of would-be naturalized citizens from five to 14 years. Another, written to expire in 1790, allowed the president to deport any alien deemed "dangerous to the peace and safety of the United States."[4] A third, the Alien Enemies Act—still in force today—permits arrest and deportation of aliens when their native countries are at war with the United States.

The most controversial law, passed on July 14, was the Sedition Act, written to expire in March 1801. The act punished any "false, scandalous, and malicious writing" against the U.S. government or its officers.[5] President Thomas Jefferson denounced the Sedition Act as unconstitutional, yet he declined to veto the law when it reached his desk. U.S. marshals were required to arrest anyone who criticized the federal government, and juries went on to convict them, whereupon Jefferson pardoned all those convicted.

The Alien and Sedition Acts passed Congress during a "quasi-war" between the United States and France, which included naval battles on various oceans worldwide. Wartime hysteria encouraged unduly harsh measures, and U.S. marshals bore the brunt of public anger in the form of protests raised by civil libertarians over civil rights violations.

DEFENDING SLAVERY

Congress also tried for decades to avoid civil war over slavery, drafting one compromise after another, striving in vain to please both sides of the explosive controversy. One such measure, passed in September 1850, was the Fugitive Slave Act, which required U.S. marshals to help slave owners capture slaves who escaped into northern free states. Failure to obey the law exposed marshals to lawsuits and severe financial penalties.

In fact, the U.S. Constitution recognized slavery's legality. Section 2 of Article I let slave states count three-fifths of each slave when calculating population to determine representation in Congress. Section 9 of Article I permitted importation of slaves from foreign countries until 1808, with Washington collecting $10 a head. Section 9 of

Article 4 concerned runaway slaves, stating that "No Person held to Service or Labour in one State, under the Laws thereof, escaping into another, shall, in Consequence of any Law or Regulation therein, be discharged from such Service or Labour, but shall be delivered upon Claim of the Party to whom such Service or Labour may be due."

Even so, the Fugitive Slave Act raised a storm of controversy that endured until the outbreak of the Civil War. It also cost the life of Deputy Marshal James Batchelder in Boston, as described above.

LIQUOR WARS

Congress resumed taxing liquor in 1862, to raise money for the Civil War, although the tax remains in place today. Of all the jobs performed by U.S. marshals throughout history, pursuing liquor tax evaders has been the most dangerous. Between 1869 and 1935, moonshiners and smugglers killed 52 deputy marshals in 13 states and Puerto Rico—nearly one-fourth of all duty-related deaths suffered by members of the Marshals Service since 1794.[6]

Hunting tax evaders was dangerous enough, but U.S. marshals were saddled with more booze problems after World War I. Congress passed the Eighteenth Amendment to the Constitution in December 1917, banning alcoholic beverages completely, one year after ratification—which occurred on January 16, 1919. Ten months later, on October 27, the Volstead Act imposed federal penalties for the manufacture, sale, or importation of liquor, wine, and beer. The law took effect at midnight on January 16, 1920, and within an hour, gangsters stole $100,000 worth of whiskey from a Chicago railroad yard.[7]

Prohibition spanned 13 years, during which America was flooded with illegal alcohol, outlawed saloons flourished, and local gangs fought bloody turf wars before creating the first national crime syndicate (a coalition of bootleggers and other gangsters formed to reduce bloodshed and increase profits from bootlegging, organized over time between 1927 and 1932). Liquor wars claimed the lives of at least 512 federal agents—including seven deputy U.S. marshals—and 2,089 suspected liquor violators by the end of 1932.[8] The final tally of gangsters and bystanders killed nationwide will never be known.

U.S. marshals shared the task of Prohibition enforcement with local police and agents of the Treasury Department's Prohibition Unit. The

BASS REEVES (1838–1910)

Bass Reeves was born into slavery in Paris, Texas, and took the surname of his master—farmer and state legislator George Reeves. Shortly before the outbreak of the Civil War, Bass beat his master in a fistfight and fled to the Indian Territory (now Oklahoma), where he lived as a fugitive with the Creek tribes until the Emancipation Proclamation freed all former slaves in territory occupied by Union troops. After the war, Reeves bought land in Arkansas and became a prosperous rancher. He also married and fathered 10 children.

Life changed for Reeves in May 1875, when Judge Isaac Parker was appointed to the federal court in Fort Smith, Arkansas. Parker chose James Fagan as his U.S. marshal and ordered him to hire 200 deputies. One of those deputies was Bass Reeves, picked as America's first black deputy U.S. marshal because he knew the Indian Territory and spoke several Native American languages. Reeves held that post for 32 years, arresting more than 3,000 felons and killing 14 in gunfights. Reeves himself was never wounded, although his belt and hat were shot off in two separate duels.[9]

With regard to those he killed, Reeves insisted that he "never shot a man when it was not necessary for him to do so in the discharge of his duty to save his own life."[10] One such man was Bob Dozier, a criminal jack-of-all-trades who rustled livestock; robbed banks, stores, and stagecoaches; "fenced" stolen jewelry; and practiced land fraud. Dozier eluded lawmen for years, until Reeves ran him to ground in Oklahoma's Cherokee Hills on December 20, 1878. Dozier refused to surrender and reached for his gun—a fatal mistake when facing Bass Reeves.

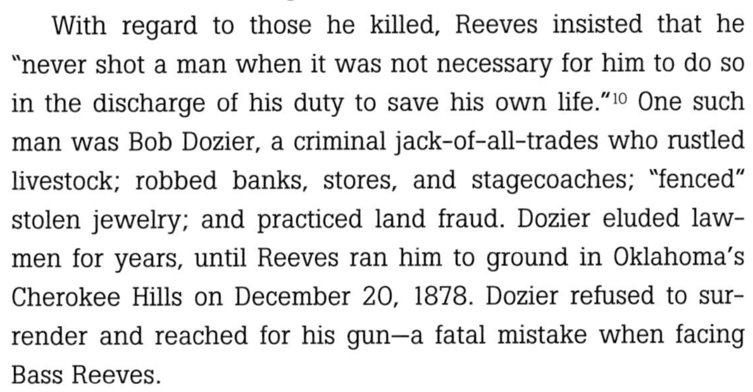

Deputy Reeves retired from federal service in 1907, when Oklahoma achieved statehood, to join Muskogee's police department. He died from Bright's disease—a kidney ailment—on January 12, 1910, and was buried in Muskogee, although the exact location of his grave is unknown today.

FREEDOM RIDES

In 1946 the U.S. Supreme Court banned racially segregated seating on interstate buses. Eighteen "freedom riders"—nine African American, nine white—boarded a southbound bus in 1947 and were jailed for sharing "white" terminal restrooms in North Carolina. Southern bus depots were still segregated in 1960, when another court ruling (*Boynton v. Virginia*) banned whites-only facilities in interstate transportation.

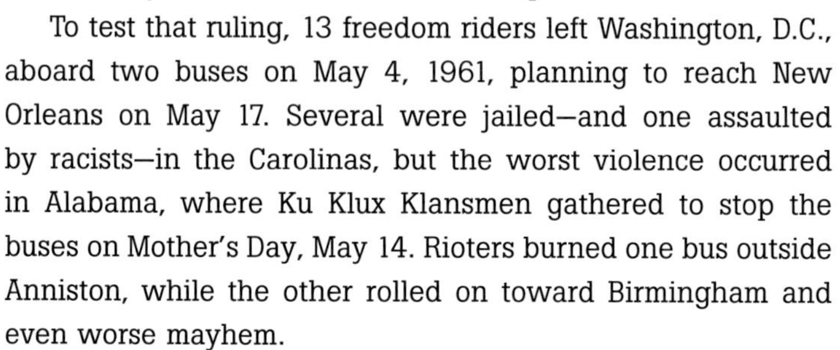

To test that ruling, 13 freedom riders left Washington, D.C., aboard two buses on May 4, 1961, planning to reach New Orleans on May 17. Several were jailed—and one assaulted by racists—in the Carolinas, but the worst violence occurred in Alabama, where Ku Klux Klansmen gathered to stop the buses on Mother's Day, May 14. Rioters burned one bus outside Anniston, while the other rolled on toward Birmingham and even worse mayhem.

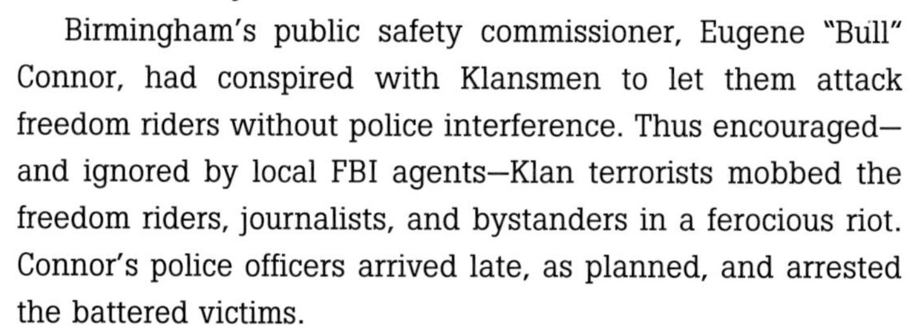

Birmingham's public safety commissioner, Eugene "Bull" Connor, had conspired with Klansmen to let them attack freedom riders without police interference. Thus encouraged—and ignored by local FBI agents—Klan terrorists mobbed the freedom riders, journalists, and bystanders in a ferocious riot. Connor's police officers arrived late, as planned, and arrested the battered victims.

U.S. Marshals Service Web site claims that marshals stopped chasing bootleggers in 1927 (when the Treasury Department formed an independent Bureau of Prohibition), but public records show that five deputy marshals died pursuing liquor violators between 1929 and 1933, and a sixth was killed by moonshiners in 1935, two years after Prohibition's repeal.[11]

SEDITION REVISITED

World War I began in August 1914, but America played no direct role until April 1917, when Congress declared war on Germany and the Austro-Hungarian Empire. Two months later, Congress passed the Espionage Act, which punished traditional spying and imposed a

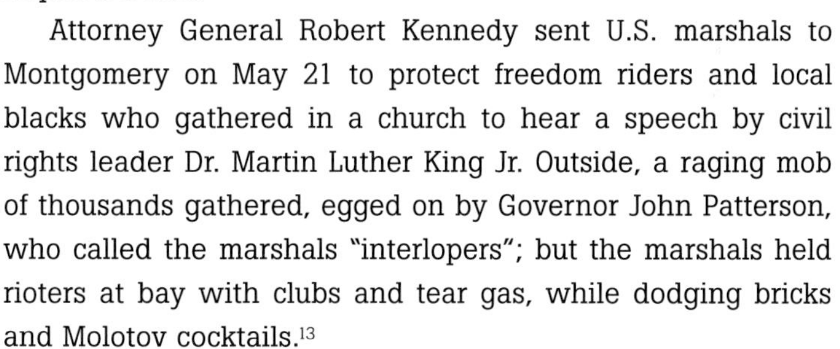

Refusing to be halted by violence, more freedom riders came south, and they faced a suspiciously similar Birmingham riot on May 19. Escorted to Montgomery by state police on May 20, the riders disembarked into another Klan riot, with police nowhere in sight. John Seigenthaler, a Justice Department observer, was beaten unconscious, then denied an ambulance because, Montgomery's police commissioner said, "He has not requested one."[12]

Attorney General Robert Kennedy sent U.S. marshals to Montgomery on May 21 to protect freedom riders and local blacks who gathered in a church to hear a speech by civil rights leader Dr. Martin Luther King Jr. Outside, a raging mob of thousands gathered, egged on by Governor John Patterson, who called the marshals "interlopers"; but the marshals held rioters at bay with clubs and tear gas, while dodging bricks and Molotov cocktails.[13]

The freedom rides finally proceeded, with more arrests in Mississippi, and legal cases dragged on for decades. In 1975, when the bureau's Klan informers had furnished proof of the Alabama riot conspiracy, injured riders James Peck and Walter Bergman sued the FBI for failure to protect them. In 1983 and 1984 Peck and Bergman received $25,000 and $35,000, respectively, for their injuries.[14]

20-year sentence on anyone convicted of making "false reports or false statements with intent to interfere with the operation or success of the military or naval forces of the United States or . . . to cause or attempt to cause insubordination, disloyalty, mutiny, refusal of duty, in the military or naval forces of the United States, or to willfully obstruct the recruiting or enlistment service of the United States."[15]

In May 1918 Congress passed an amendment to that law, commonly called the Sedition Act. That amendment imposed the same 20-year sentence on anyone who

> shall willfully utter, print, write or publish any disloyal, profane, scurrilous, or abusive language about the form of government

> of the United States or the Constitution of the United States, or the military or naval forces of the United States, or the flag of the United States, or the uniform of the Army or Navy of the United States into contempt, scorn, contumely, or disrepute, or shall willfully utter, print, write, or publish any language intended to incite, provoke, or encourage resistance to the United States, or to promote the cause of its enemies.[16]

Once again, freedom of speech was sacrificed to wartime hysteria, with U.S. marshals required to enforce the harsh laws. Socialist Party leader Eugene Debs received a 10-year sentence for opposing military conscription. Poet E. E. Cummings was arrested in September 1917, while serving as a volunteer ambulance driver in France, simply for saying that he did not hate Germans. In the United States, 2,000 defendants faced trial and 75 newspapers lost their mailing privileges for criticizing the war or draft. None were foreign spies.[17]

U.S. marshals took the heat for those arrests, but they carried on in spite of mounting criticism. The original Espionage Act expired at war's end, in November 1918. Congress repealed the Sedition Act in December 1920, after numerous complaints about abusive prosecutions.

CIVIL RIGHTS AND WRONGS

After granting citizenship to ex-slaves in the Reconstruction era (1865–76), Congress abandoned African Americans to 80 years of racial segregation, loss of voting rights, and terrorism from lynch mobs. The U.S. Supreme Court reversed that trend in 1954, banning segregation in public schools, but years of violence and protest followed before nonwhites achieved something resembling full equality.

Congress lagged behind the court, passing its first civil rights law in 82 years during August 1957. Other laws followed, dismantling a system of legalized discrimination that spanned the nation, affecting Hispanics, Asians, and Native Americans, as well as blacks.

Since J. Edgar Hoover's FBI refused to act in civil rights cases without direct presidential orders—and, even then, agents would not protect civil rights activists from attack by racist police or vigilantes—U.S. marshals were America's frontline troops in the struggle for civil rights. They received their baptism by fire during the Alabama "freedom rides" of 1961, but worse violence flared the following year, when black student James Meredith enrolled at the all-white University of Mississippi.

State officials blocked Meredith's admission to "Ole Miss" for months, finally surrendering when threatened with jail for contempt

James Meredith *(center, with briefcase)* is escorted to the University of Mississippi campus in Oxford on October 2, 1962, by Chief U.S. Marshal James McShane *(left)* and an unidentified marshal *(right)*. *(AP Photo)*

of a federal court. Next, racist groups broadcast a call for volunteers to gather at the university and physically prevent Meredith's enrollment. Expecting violence, President John Kennedy sent marshals to the university campus in Oxford to protect Meredith's rights and life.

Rioting on campus began at 10:00 P.M. on September 30, 1962, and continued until 5:30 A.M. on October 1, when U.S. troops arrived to occupy Oxford. Meanwhile, 300 deputy mashals armed with revolvers, nightsticks, and tear gas faced a mob of thousands firing rifles and shotguns, hurling firebombs, and charging the marshals' ranks with vehicles, including a fire truck and a bulldozer. Local police made no arrests—and some joined in the rioting—but most of those involved in what historian William Doyle calls "a Ku Klux Klan rebellion" were students or racist vigilantes.[18]

When the smoke cleared, two civilians were dead, 375 were injured, and marshals had arrested 300. Of the marshals at Ole Miss, 166 were injured, 30 by gunfire. Deputy Marshal Graham Same nearly died from a sniper's shot to the throat. Most of those arrested were released without charges. Only four—all from out of state—faced trial, and all were acquitted by white juries after their attorneys accused marshals of beating them in custody. Chooky Fowler, commander of Oxford's National Guard unit, denied those claims, saying, "I was there. It didn't happen." Campus chaplain Wofford Smith told journalists, "Those marshals were the bravest men I ever saw."[19]

WOUNDED KNEE

A different kind of racial conflict began on February 27, 1973, when armed members of the American Indian Movement (AIM) occupied Wounded Knee, South Dakota, the site of the last battle in America's Indian wars, where soldiers killed 300 men, women, and children in 1890. AIM members chose the site for their protest against broken treaties and poverty suffered by residents of America's Indian reservations.

Members of the U.S. Marshals Service joined FBI agents to patrol Wounded Knee, located on the Pine Ridge Indian Reservation, during a 71-day siege that ended on May 8, 1973. The standoff included several

With a double-barreled shotgun *(foreground)* ready, U.S. marshals watch activity in the brush near Wounded Knee, South Dakota, on April 13, 1973. *(Bettmann/Corbis)*

shootouts between AIM members and federal officers, including members of the U.S. Marshals' Special Operations Group (SOG). On one occasion, SOG officers rescued six FBI agents who were pinned down by AIM snipers. They also took hits of their own—Deputy Marshal Lloyd Grimm was paralyzed for life.

Resolution of the Wounded Knee incident did not end conflicts between AIM and the U.S. government. Violence continued at Pine Ridge for two years, much of it traced to a vigilante group called Guardians of the Oglala Nation, which AIM members say was armed and financed by the FBI. In June 1975 two FBI agents and an AIM member died in another battle at Pine Ridge. Agents arrested three AIM members, but jurors acquitted two of them at trial. The third, Leonard Peltier, received a double term of life imprisonment. Some critics still maintain that he was framed.[20]

GUARDING THE CAPITAL

U.S. marshals are called out for duty whenever riots or protest demonstrations threaten federal property in Washington, D.C. That service, since the 1960s, has placed them in opposition to rioting African Americans, antiwar protesters, and members of the modern Ku Klux Klan.

In April 1968, after a sniper killed Dr. Martin Luther King Jr. in Tennessee, riots erupted in black ghettos across the United States. By mid-May, at least 125 cities had suffered mob violence and 46 people had lost their lives. In Washington, between April 4 and April 8, some 20,000 rioters overwhelmed the city's 3,100-member police force, prompting President Lyndon Johnson to mobilize U.S. marshals and 13,600 soldiers. Rioters came within two blocks of the White House, and the final toll was grim: 12 dead, 1,097 injured, and more than 6,100 arrested. At least 1,200 buildings were burned, with damages valued at $27 million ($156 million today).[21]

Marshals in War and Peace

Bell's Canyon, Arizona

Congress created Arizona's Colorado River Indian Reservation—spanning 432 square miles of La Paz County, Arizona, and neighboring California—in March 1865. Former California state legislator George Leihy was named as its superintendent, governing members of the Chemehuevi, Hopi, Mojave, and Navajo tribes. Leihy also served as deputy U.S. marshal for his judicial district, operating from La Paz.

Most accounts describe Leihy as a compassionate man who was active in attempts to support and expand tribal agriculture. Still, he managed to offend some tribesmen on the reservation, where two white prospectors had been killed at Skull Valley, between La Paz and Prescott, in 1894. In the autumn of 1866, friends warned Leihy of a tribal plot against his life, but Leihy ignored them. On November 18, while returning to La Paz from Prescott, Leihy and his clerk were ambushed and killed in Skull Valley.

According to historian Thomas Farish, "Their bodies were horribly mangled. His murderers at once returned to the reservation and spread the news, whereupon for two days and nights there was great rejoicing among the tribe. Horses were killed and eaten, as was their custom on their days of feasting or celebration."[1] Deputy Leihy's murder went unpunished, and Arizona's Indian wars continued for another 20 years.

DEFENDING AMERICA

U.S. marshals are not military officers, but their duties frequently expand during wartime, as they enforce new laws passed by Congress to deal with emergencies. Marshals were required to enforce the Alien and Sedition Acts of 1798, passed during America's undeclared "quasi-war" against France. Parts of those laws were unconstitutional, but that judgment is left to the courts, while marshals must perform their duties or face dismissal and harsh penalties.

During the War of 1812, aliens residing in America were ordered to register with the U.S. marshals in their districts. Again, the marshals did their best, but only 10,000 aliens were counted before the war's end, when the order expired.[2] Meanwhile, Marshal Peter Duplessis pursued French pirates in Louisiana, while other marshals distinguished themselves in battle.

After serving as Maine's first U.S. marshal, Henry Dearborn served in Congress from 1793 to 1797, then as President Jefferson's secretary of war from 1801 to 1809 and revenue collector for the port of Boston from 1809 to 1812. When Congress declared war on Britain in June 1812, Dearborn re-entered military service as a major general of the U.S. Army, planning a two-pronged invasion of Canada. Those efforts failed, and he finished the war as president of the court-martial that sentenced General William Hull to die for losing Detroit to British troops. President James Madison pardoned Hull, and tried to reappoint Dearborn as secretary of war, but the Senate rejected his nomination.

Lewis Cass (1782–1866) served as Ohio's U.S. marshal from 1807 to 1813, when he assumed the rank of brigadier general and participated in the Battle of the Thames, near Chatham, Ontario, in October 1813. American forces defeated British troops and hostile tribesmen, killing Shawnee war chief Tecumseh, and President Madison rewarded Cass with an appointment as governor of the Michigan Territory. Cass held that post until August 1831, when he resigned to serve as President Andrew Jackson's secretary of war. Cass was also America's ambassador to France from 1836 to 1842 and represented Michigan in the U.S. Senate from 1845 to 1857.

CIVIL WAR

Between December 1860 and May 1861, 11 slave states left the Union to form the Confederate States of America. Secession removed those

DEFENDING NEW ORLEANS

Peter Duplessis was appointed to serve as the fourth U.S. marshal of the Louisiana Territory on April 30, 1811. Territorial Governor William Claiborne opposed his appointment, instead nominating a personal friend for the job, but Attorney General Caesar Rodney supported Duplessis. One year later, to the day, Louisiana was admitted to the Union as the 15th state.

Marshal Duplessis spent his first year in office pursuing brothers Jean and Pierre Lafitte, pirates who operated from New Orleans until 1807, then shifted their base to an island in Barataria Bay, off Louisiana's southeastern coast. By 1812, with a private fleet and 1,000 men, the Lafittes raided shipping vessels throughout the Gulf of Mexico, "taxing" any ship that entered the Mississippi River. Attacks on Spanish ships threatened America's relationship with Spain, but worse trouble erupted in June 1812, when the United States declared war on Britain.

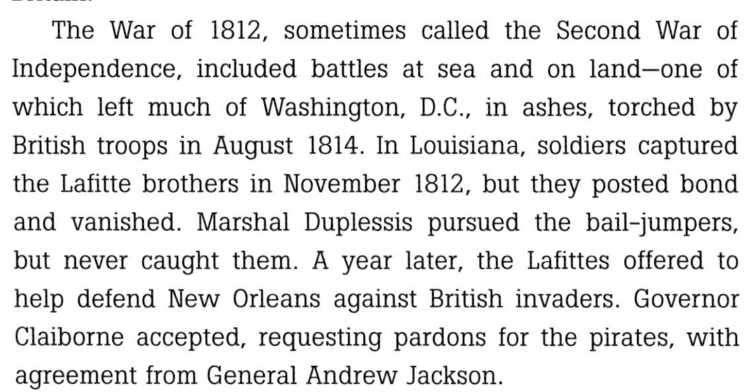

The War of 1812, sometimes called the Second War of Independence, included battles at sea and on land—one of which left much of Washington, D.C., in ashes, torched by British troops in August 1814. In Louisiana, soldiers captured the Lafitte brothers in November 1812, but they posted bond and vanished. Marshal Duplessis pursued the bail-jumpers, but never caught them. A year later, the Lafittes offered to help defend New Orleans against British invaders. Governor Claiborne accepted, requesting pardons for the pirates, with agreement from General Andrew Jackson.

The Treaty of Ghent officially ended hostilities between America and Britain in December 1814, but the news was slow to reach Louisiana. On January 8, 1815, General Jackson and Jean Lafitte killed 1,784 British invaders at the Battle of New Orleans, while losing only 210 of their own men.[3] That belated triumph made Jackson a hero and won him the presidency in 1828. Meanwhile, the Lafittes continued on as buccaneers and agents of Spain during the Mexican War of Independence. Pierre died fighting rebels in Mexico in 1821. Jean died in battle against Spanish pirates in February 1823.

states from federal control, and also canceled the commissions of U.S. marshals serving in rebel districts. Above the Mason-Dixon Line, those marshals who remained chased counterfeiters and Confederate spies, seized property used to support the rebellion, and one—Deputy Ward Lamon—served as personal bodyguard to President Abraham Lincoln.

Other past and future U.S. marshals served in uniform on both sides of the conflict. Pennsylvania native Francis Herron (1837–1902) won a Congressional Medal of Honor for his bravery at the Battle of Pea Ridge, Arkansas, in March 1862, and went on to become the Union army's youngest major general. During Reconstruction he served as a deputy U.S. marshal in New Orleans from 1867 to 1869 and as Louisiana's secretary of state in 1872 and 1873.

Another Pennsylvania native, Richard Griffith (1814–62), moved to Mississippi after the Mexican War and served as deputy U.S. marshal for that state's southern district from 1853 to 1857. He joined the 12th Mississippi Infantry as a colonel in May 1861, and was promoted to brigadier general in December. Griffith died in the Battle of Savage's Station, Virginia, in June 1862.

Benjamin McCulloch (1811–62) followed Tennessee legend Davy Crockett to Texas in 1835, and while illness kept him from dying with Crockett at the Alamo, he helped avenge that slaughter in the April 1836 Battle of San Jacinto. He then joined the Texas Rangers, fought in the Mexican War (1846–48), and served as a deputy U.S. marshal in Texas from 1852 through 1860. When Texas seceded in February 1861, McCullough joined the Confederate army as a colonel. He died at the Battle of Pea Ridge in March 1862.

Ben McCulloch's younger brother, Henry (1816–95), also served as a deputy marshal in Texas from 1857 to 1861, and then as a brigadier general in the Confederate army. He survived the war and entered Texas politics, appointed as superintendent of Austin's Deaf and Dumb Asylum in 1876. Mismanagement forced his resignation in 1879, and he retired from public life.

Another prewar marshal, Tennessee native James Patton Anderson (1822–72), served in the Washington Territory before joining a Confederate army unit from Florida as a colonel in 1861. By 1864 he was a major general, commanding all troops in Florida until its capture by the Union. After the war, Anderson became the editor of a newspaper.

Appointed U.S. marshal for the District of Columbia by Abraham Lincoln in 1861, Ward Hill Lamon later served as Lincoln's personal bodyguard. He resigned as marshal after Lincoln's assassination. *(Kean Collection/Getty Images)*

At least three other Confederate veterans served as deputy U.S. marshals after the Civil War. Kentucky native Thomas Hart Taylor (1825–1901) entered service as a captain and finished the war as provost marshal of Mobile, Alabama. After the war, he returned to Kentucky and spent five years as a deputy marshal, followed by 11 years as Louisville's police chief.

William Wirt Allen (1835–94) was born in New York, but he joined Alabama forces as a lieutenant in 1861, rising to the rank of major general by 1865. He remained in Alabama following the war, serving as a deputy U.S. marshal and as the state's adjutant general under President Grover Cleveland.

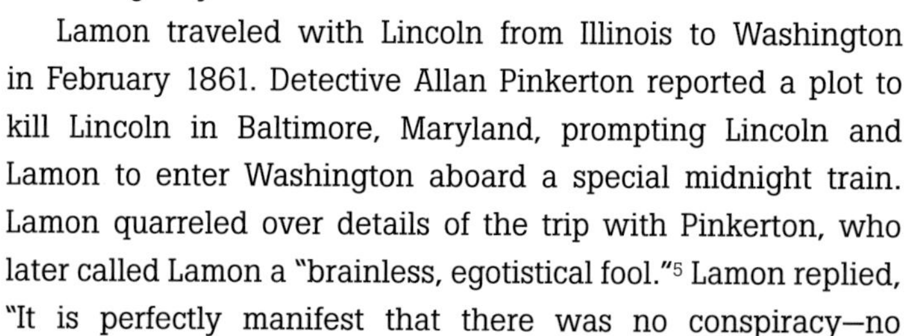

WARD HILL LAMON (1828–93)

A Virginia native, Ward Lamon studied medicine for two years before moving to Illinois at age 19. There, he switched to legal studies, was admitted to the state bar in 1851, and entered partnership with Abraham Lincoln at Danville the following year. Their partnership ended in 1857, when Lamon became a prosecutor and moved to Bloomsbury, but their friendship endured despite strong disagreements on the subject of slavery. Although Lincoln was an abolitionist and Lamon favored slavery, Lamon campaigned for Lincoln and the anti-slavery Republican Party in 1860. When Lincoln won the presidency, he asked Lamon to join him in Washington and "be prepared for a long stay."[4]

Lamon traveled with Lincoln from Illinois to Washington in February 1861. Detective Allan Pinkerton reported a plot to kill Lincoln in Baltimore, Maryland, prompting Lincoln and Lamon to enter Washington aboard a special midnight train. Lamon quarreled over details of the trip with Pinkerton, who later called Lamon a "brainless, egotistical fool."[5] Lamon replied, "It is perfectly manifest that there was no conspiracy—no

Bryan Morel Thomas (1836–1905) graduated from West Point in 1858 and then resigned from the U.S. Army to serve his native Georgia in April 1861. Rising from the rank of lieutenant to brigadier general by August 1864, he served as a deputy U.S. marshal in postwar Georgia, founded a private academy in 1884, and then served as superintendent of schools in Dalton, Georgia.

RECONSTRUCTION

The Confederate surrender in April 1865 did not end armed hostilities in the South. During Reconstruction, racist groups such as the Ku Klux Klan terrorized former slaves and any whites who supported black citizenship. U.S. marshals in the South pursued racist terrorists, captured many, and maintained security when they were brought to trial in federal

conspiracy of a hundred, of fifty, of twenty, of three; no definite purpose in the heart of even one man to murder Mr. Lincoln in Baltimore."[6]

In March 1861 Lincoln appointed Lamon as U.S. marshal for the District of Columbia. Lamon visited Fort Sumter, South Carolina, days before its shelling by Confederate artillery started the Civil War, and later served as Lincoln's personal bodyguard, although that duty did not fall within a marshal's jurisdiction. Lamon spent most nights at the White House patrolling the grounds and sometimes slept outside the door to Lincoln's bedroom. Sadly, he was on assignment in Richmond, Virginia, when Lincoln was shot at Ford's Theater by John Wilkes Booth on April 14, 1865. Grief-stricken, Lamon accompanied Lincoln's funeral procession, and then resigned as marshal in June, declining appointment as postmaster general under President Andrew Johnson.

In later life, Lamon wrote two books about Lincoln and practiced law until 1879. He then traveled widely until his wife died in Europe in 1892. Lamon then lived with his daughter in West Virginia until his death in May 1893.

court. It was dangerous duty, as Klansmen killed thousands of ex-slaves and white carpetbaggers, with no respect for law enforcement officers.

Deputy Marshal R. T. Dunn served in Mississippi, where some of the Klan's worst violence was perpetrated. With two other marshals, Dunn arrested several Klansmen for assault in July 1873, after which the other deputies left Mississippi, leaving Dunn to complete the investigation. On August 8, 1873, one of the suspects arrested by Dunn—free on bail—invaded Dunn's rooming house in Corinth, Mississippi, and shot him dead in his room.[7]

Eleven months later, in Tennessee, Deputy Marshal James Everette met a similar fate at the hands of Klansmen. Everette was serving federal arrest warrants around Lynchburg on July 10, 1874, when he was ambushed by Klan members. Investigators thought that he had fallen from his horse and suffered injury, at which time Klansmen shot him twice and destroyed his warrants. Deputy Everette's killers were never punished.[8]

WORLD WAR I

Aside from enforcement of the Espionage and Sedition Acts, U.S. marshals performed numerous war-related duties during World War I. In April 1917 alone, they ordered Germans living in America to surrender all weapons, explosives, and radios, arresting those who refused; jailed specific "enemy aliens"—natives of countries at war with America—named in federal warrants and delivered them to the War Department for incarceration; and guarded various arsenals, docks, factories, and other critical facilities, issuing passes to aliens permitted access as workers.

May 1917 saw marshals assigned to guard Selective Service offices; they also arrested draft evaders and anyone who opposed conscription. In October marshals got the added job of tracking down military deserters. November brought orders to remove all enemy aliens from Washington, D.C., and report their arrival in other districts. In December 1917 marshals were ordered to identify all male German-Americans in cities of 5,000 persons or more. January 1918 expanded that task to include registration of all enemy aliens at local post offices, while helping those unemployed to find jobs. Registration of female enemy aliens followed in April 1918.

During America's 17 months of war, U.S. marshals investigated 222,768 violations of the Selective Service laws, jailed 6,300 enemy aliens under presidential arrest warrants, interviewed 2,300 in military detention camps, registered 480,000 German Americans nationwide, and issued 200,000 permits for enemy aliens to enter restricted areas.[9]

WORLD WAR II

As in World War I, the United States avoided direct participation in the next global conflict for as long as deemed possible. The Japanese bombing of Pearl Harbor, Hawaii, on December 7, 1941, finally prompted a declaration of war against the Axis Powers—Germany, Italy, and Japan—followed by full-scale mobilization for war.

This time, aided by local police, the FBI did most of America's domestic spy hunting, while U.S. marshals resumed their role of monitoring and arresting enemy aliens. In World War II, however, scrutiny was not restricted to Germans. In January 1942 Attorney General Francis Biddle told the *New York Times* that 1,102,000 enemy aliens were known to live in the United States, including 695,000 Italians, 315,000 Germans, and 92,000 Japanese.[10] None of those figures were accurate, and confusion still surrounds some ensuing events.

Treatment of enemy aliens varied, depending on race and location. The Alien Act of 1798—still in force today—permits internment (detention) when war is declared or a foreign invasion is threatened. While thousands were confined to special camps guarded by military personnel, others were forcibly removed and banned from "military zones" comprising more than one-third of the United States.

Restrictions began in December 1941 as enemy aliens in the United States, Puerto Rico, and the Virgin Islands received orders to surrender all cameras, radio transmitters, and short-wave receivers. A month later, President Franklin Roosevelt ordered all enemy aliens 14 or older to register at their nearest post office. In February Executive Order 9066 allowed the secretary of war to define military zones wherein "the right of any person to enter, remain in or leave shall be subject to whatever restrictions" deemed necessary.[11]

In March 1942 President Roosevelt created the War Relocation Authority as a means to manage the removal of enemy aliens from designated military zones. Within a few months, federal agents had arrested 1,521 Italians, 250 of whom spent the next 14 months in military prison camps. Roughly 11,000 Germans—including some born in the United States—were also interned. Japanese suffered the most, with 1,200 interned in Hawaii and about 110,000 confined to camps in the western United States. Sixty-two percent of the Japanese confined were U.S. citizens.[12]

U.S. marshals handled most of those arrests, while American progress on foreign battlefields slowly eased some regulations. Most restrictions on naturalized Italian Americans were removed in October 1942, and the rest with Italy's surrender in September 1943. Germany surrendered in May 1945. Two months later, President Harry Truman issued a proclamation allowing deportation of enemy aliens deemed "dangerous to the public peace and safety of the United States," but Japan's surrender on August 14 stalled that move. Most detainees were released by November 1945, and U.S. marshals returned to normal peacetime duties.

VIETNAM

America's long, undeclared war in Vietnam confronted U.S. marshals with the unfamiliar problem of mass protests against the nation's foreign policy. Local police handled most of the angry demonstrations, often responding with violence of their own, while the FBI placed antiwar activists under surveillance, sometimes harassing them illegally. U.S. marshals avoided the conflict unless federal property was threatened, as in October 1967.

On October 21 a crowd of some 100,000 protesters rallied at the Lincoln Memorial in Washington, D.C., for antiwar speeches delivered by Dr. Martin Luther King Jr. and Dr. Benjamin Spock. The protest began peacefully, but grew rowdier in late afternoon, as 35,000 marched on military headquarters at the Pentagon, in nearby Arlington, Virginia. There, 300 deputy marshals joined military police to prevent demonstrators from invading the restricted facility.[13]

Violence broke out as protesters pelted the marshals with fruit, rocks, and bottles. Soldiers held in reserve then appeared, to reinforce the line, and a full-scale riot erupted, lasting well into the night. Before peace was restored, 47 persons on both sides were injured, with 682 arrested.[14] Among those jailed was author Norman Mailer, whose novel describing the protest—*The Armies of the Night* (1968)—won both a Pulitzer Prize and a National Book Award.

DESERT STORM

Another controversial and divisive conflict was the Persian Gulf War of 1990–91, also known as "Operation Desert Storm." While President George H. W. Bush maintained that military force was necessary to defend Kuwait from Iraqi invaders, critics at home described the campaign as a grab for Middle Eastern oil. Protests resulted, forcing U.S. marshals once again to hold the line against trespass on federal property.

During the first three weeks of Desert Storm, deputy U.S. marshals secured federal buildings nationwide during 80 protest demonstrations. The largest were in San Francisco (where an estimated 30,000 antiwar activists gathered and 431 were arrested) and in Los Angeles (where a smaller rally produced 158 arrests). Chief Deputy Marshal Richard Bippus suffered a broken ankle at the San Francisco demonstration, but

Deputy U.S. Marshal Paul McErlean, in the front seat, conducts a security mission over Baghdad, Iraq, with other deputies in 2006. McErlean and his colleagues were in the country to train Iraqis to secure the integrity of a justice system previously riddled with corruption and fear. *(AP Photo/U.S. Marshals)*

protests against Desert Storm never attained the scope or violence of those against the Vietnam War.[15]

THE IRAQ WAR

The U.S. Marshals faced new wartime responsibilities after America's second invasion of Iraq, in March 2003. Deputy marshals escorted deposed Iraqi dictator Saddam Hussein to his trial in Baghdad (resulting in his execution by hanging), and have trained Iraqi police to improve their professional standards. Courthouse bombings and shootings in Iraq require around-the-clock security, with high risk to the marshals and their allies. One who paid the ultimate price was a native Iraqi interpreter employed by marshals in Baghdad, murdered by guerillas after nearly a year of service.[16]

Witness Security Program (WITSEC)

Savannah, Georgia

When a heart attack killed Thomas Neil Moore in May 1998, few Savannah, Georgia, residents noticed. Moore was bankrupt and $60,000 in debt, with few friends to mourn his passing.[1] Then, five months later, his death made surprising headlines nationwide.

"Moore" had once been Gary Thomas Rowe, a member of the Alabama Ku Klux Klan who doubled as an FBI informant. In 1961 he tipped agents to a plot between Birmingham police and Klansmen to attack "freedom riders," then joined in the riots himself. Four years later, he was present when Klansmen shot civil rights worker Viola Liuzzo. After that crime, Rowe broke cover to testify at several trials, wherein the killers were acquitted of murder and then convicted on civil rights charges.

Facing death threats from the Klan, Rowe received a new identity and joined the U.S. Marshals Service in January 1966. His tenure in San Diego, California, lasted until November 1967, when a series of drunken brawls—including one fight with a federal courthouse janitor—forced his resignation.

Rowe resurfaced in 1975, testifying at Senate hearings on the FBI's illegal counterintelligence activities during the 1960s, then dropped

FBI agents surround informer Gary Thomas Rowe as he leaves a courthouse after testifying in the trial of one of civil rights worker Viola Liuzzo's murderers. In a strange turn of events, Rowe was later employed by the U.S. Marshals Service after entering the Witness Security Program. *(Francis Miller/Time Life Pictures/Getty)*

from public view once more, until his death. Today, some researchers claim that Rowe himself shot Liuzzo in 1965, and others suggest his involvement in a 1963 bombing that killed four girls in a Birmingham, Alabama, church. Whatever the truth of those claims, Rowe took the answers to his grave in 1998—and in the process, embarrassed the Marshals Service one last time.

NEW NAMES, NEW LIVES

The federal program to protect endangered witnesses dates from 1871, when members of the first Ku Klux Klan killed anyone likely to testify against them in court. Later efforts to safeguard federal witnesses were haphazard. Some witnesses, like Mafia turncoat Joseph Valachi (1903–71), were concealed on military bases. Others were guarded in hotels or shipped to cities far from home. Gary Rowe is, according to information currently available, the only witness to have been placed on the U.S. Marshals Service payroll with a badge and gun.

Congress tackled racketeering in 1970 with the Organized Crime Control Act. Title V of that law—"Protected Facilities for Housing Government Witnesses"—allowed the attorney general to protect federal witnesses in "whatever manner deemed most useful under the special circumstances of each case." Thus was born the federal Witness Security Program—"WITSEC" for short. In 1984 the Comprehensive Crime Control Act extended protection to relatives or associates of endangered witnesses.

According to the Marshals Service, WITSEC has admitted more than 8,200 witnesses and some 9,800 family members since 1971. While protection under WITSEC is not dependent on conviction of accused defendants, service spokesmen note that 89 percent of those who face protected witnesses in court have been convicted and imprisoned.[2]

DISAPPEARING ACTS

To enter WITSEC, a potential witness must possess vital information in a criminal or civil case awaiting trial, and there must be a serious threat to the witness's life. Federal prosecutors recommend admission to the program, which must be cleared by the Department of Justice with final approval from the U.S. attorney general.

Once approval is granted, WITSEC subjects receive pre-admittance counseling from U.S. marshals. The program's rules are explained in detail, and subjects must agree in writing to obey them, creating a legal contract. Failure to abide by any rules—obeying all laws, avoiding contact with former associates, and so on—may lead to expulsion from the program.

Upon entering WITSEC, each subject receives a new identity, complete with documentation such as birth certificates, Social Security cards, driver's licenses, and high school or college transcripts. While described by the Marshals Service as "authentic," these documents support false identities.[3] Plastic surgery is *not* provided to alter a subject's appearance, although stories persist that some women in WITSEC have demanded various cosmetic operations.[4]

Contrary to the claims of some defense attorneys, WITSEC subjects are not paid to testify in court. Housing, medical care, and subsistence funding are provided to cover basic living expenses until subjects become self-supporting. To that end, when forced to abandon their jobs, subjects may be placed in temporary jobs and offered training for new careers. A doctor placed in WITSEC, for example, may be barred from exposing himself to enemies by practicing medicine in his new life.

An exception to those rules involves prison inmates who enter WITSEC. While some may bargain for early release and a new life in the free world, others remain incarcerated. For these protected witnesses, security is provided by the Federal Bureau of Prisons, rather than the U.S. Marshals Service. Their defense may be as simple as solitary confinement, or it may involve a prison transfer with altered records to reflect a new identity and fabricated charges.

HOW SAFE IS WITSEC?

U.S. marshals provide 24-hour protection for subjects in "high threat environments," defined as including pretrial conferences, testimony at trial, and any other court appearances.[5] Once service as a witness is completed, including any retrials or appeals, protection is relaxed. Some WITSEC subjects spend decades in the program, rarely seeing any members of the Marshals Service unless some serious problem occurs.

All WITSEC subjects are forbidden from returning to their hometowns or contacting any relatives or friends outside the program. This may prove traumatic, and has caused some subjects to leave WITSEC—a right they retain after signing their contracts. Subjects who quit the program must sign a release absolving the Marshals Service of any further duty to protect them. Service spokesmen state that "no program participant who follows security guidelines has ever been harmed while under the active protection of the Marshals Service," but no records exist for subjects who quit the program.[6]

A disturbing lapse in WITSEC security emerged in April 2009, when jurors convicted Deputy U.S. Marshal John Ambrose of leaking information about one witness to members of the Chicago Mafia. That witness—mobster Nicholas Calabrese, confessed slayer of 14 victims—was unharmed and swiftly relocated.

FBI agents cracked the Ambrose case while eavesdropping on gangsters in a prison visiting room. One gangster boasted of a "mole" (a spy within an organization who passes on information) inside the Marshals Service, and the agents started digging. Ambrose had been assigned to guard Calabrese at a federal safe house during trials that sent three Chicago gangsters to prison for life, and when confronted by the FBI, he allegedly confessed to spilling WITSEC secrets. Later, at trial, Ambrose denied any confession, leaving his attorney to portray him as an innocent bungler who "shot his mouth off" to friends, but never betrayed his oath of office. Jurors disagreed, but did acquit Ambrose on two counts of lying to FBI agents.[7]

MAX MERMELSTEIN (1942–2008)

Born in Brooklyn, Max Mermelstein graduated from New York City Community College in 1963 with a degree in mechanical engineering. Over the next 15 years he served as site manager for various hotels in New Jersey, Miami, Puerto Rico, and the Bahamas. He also married a Colombian native and learned to speak fluent Spanish. In Puerto Rico Mermelstein befriended a member of Colombia's Medellín drug cartel; he witnessed his first murder in December 1978. The gunman then told him, "You now work for me."[8]

Over the next seven years, until federal agents arrested him on June 5, 1985, Mermelstein smuggled drugs worth a total of approximately $360 million into the United States through Florida and Los Angeles, California. At his arrest, agents seized a pistol from Mermelstein's car, then moved on to search his home, where they found 25 more guns and $250,000 in cash. Indicted and facing a near-certain life sentence—or execution by his former partners—Mermelstein "rolled over" on his Colombian bosses and entered the WITSEC program. James Walsh,

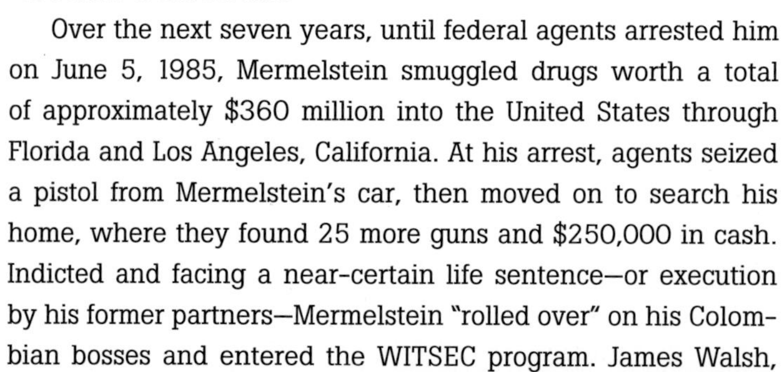

Although damage from Ambrose's lapse was averted, U.S. Attorney Gary Shapiro expressed the feelings of most federal agents when he said, "This is a real tragedy for federal law enforcement and for Deputy Marshal John Ambrose."[9] Ambrose faces a four-year prison term for leaking confidential information, and WITSEC and the Marshals Service strive to repair their damaged reputation.

STATE PROGRAMS

Aside from maintaining the federal WITSEC program, Washington also grants funds to help state governments create their own witness protection networks. While such programs are not advertised, media reports confirm that 14 states have systems that resemble WITSEC.[10] Unfortunately, when state programs do make headlines, it is often bad news.

head of the U.S. Attorney's narcotics task force in Los Angeles, called Mermelstein "probably the single most valuable government witness in drug matters in the country today. I don't think it's possible to overstate the significance of his testimony."[11]

As a protected witness, Mermelstein testified at hearings and trials in Miami, Los Angeles, and New Orleans. Dozens of drug dealers were indicted for smuggling, and for five murders spanning the years 1978 to 1985. In retaliation, cartel leaders placed a double price on Mermelstein's head: $500,000 dead in the United States, and $1 million if delivered alive to Colombia.[12]

No one ever collected that bounty, and while the cartel's top leaders remained safe in Colombia, several underlings were convicted of murder, conspiracy, and other charges and sentenced to life in prison. Mermelstein lived on in Lexington, Kentucky, under a new name provided by U.S. marshals, until cancer claimed his life at age 65 on September 12, 2008. His friends and neighbors there were shocked to learn Mermelstein's true identity.

Rachel Mosley, a drug-addicted prostitute, witnessed the murder of New York City policeman Edward Byrne in February 1988. She testified against the drug dealers responsible, sending them to prison for life, but that courageous act turned her already difficult life into a waking nightmare. Constantly threatened by other gangsters, Mosley's mother, Eddie Lou Houseal, fled New York to hide in far-off Gadsden, Alabama. When threats resumed there, she alerted local police—who arrested her, instead of the felons harassing her. Three days later, Houseal allegedly killed herself in jail by swallowing two bars of soap. Local prosecutors absolved police and jailers of any wrongdoing, while Alabama's

SALVATORE GRAVANO (1945–)

Salvatore "Sammy the Bull" Gravano was born in the Bensonhurst neighborhood of Brooklyn, New York. He suffered from dyslexia, unrecognized by relatives and teachers, which led to failure and embarrassment in school. By the time he dropped out at 16, Gravano was a seasoned thief and member of a local street gang. Two years in the U.S. Army failed to reform him, and he left the service in 1966 to join New York City's Colombo crime family. Two years later, he was sworn in as an oath-bound member of the Mafia. From petty crime, he soon advanced to hijacking, loan-sharking, and contract murder, claiming his first known victim in 1970. A few years later, he switched allegiance to the larger and more powerful Gambino family.

Gravano became a prolific killer (he later confessed to 19 murders and is suspected of many others). In December 1985 he helped mobster John Gotti plan the murder of family boss Paul Castellano, which left Gotti in charge with Gravano as his right-hand man and *consiglieri* (counselor). During several Gotti trials in the late 1980s, Gravano bribed jurors to ensure his acquittal.

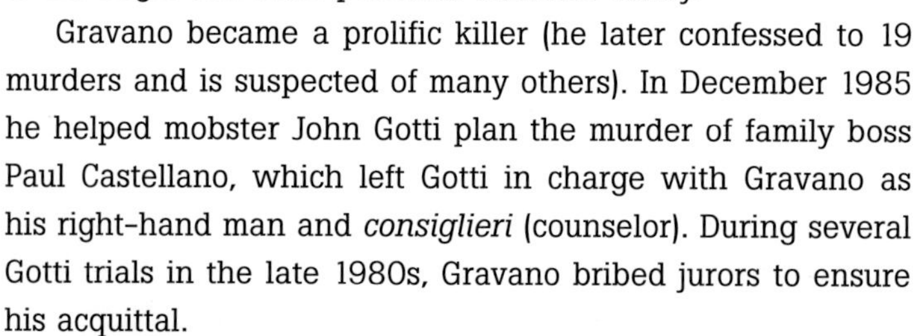

Despite their close bond, Gravano disliked Gotti's life as a "media mob star" and his portrayal as the "Teflon Don" who

medical examiner dismissed other wounds found on Houseal's body as irrelevant.[13]

Bobby Gibson witnessed the murder of a friend in New York City in August 2001, and agreed to testify against the killer (his half-brother). Prosecutors were understandably surprised at Gibson's desire to testify against his violent family member, and police provided protection. Meanwhile, the defendant intimidated other witnesses into changing their stories or flatly refusing to testify. Gibson's story would have been enough to close the case, but he never got to testify. Hours before the trial was scheduled to start, in June 2002, unknown gunmen shot and

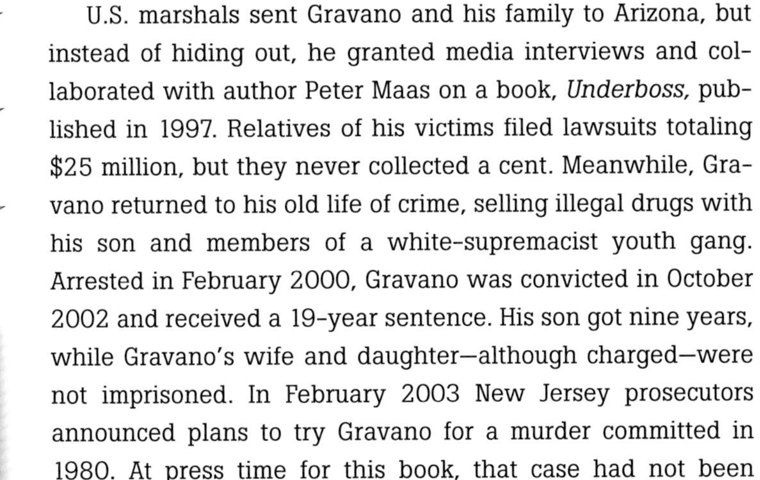

seemed untouchable. FBI agents widened the rift by letting Gravano hear conversations taped in Gotti's office in which Gotti insulted Gravano. In 1991 Gravano agreed to testify against Gotti and other mobsters. Thanks to him, jurors convicted Gotti of racketeering in April 1992. He received a life sentence and died in prison 10 years later. Despite his confession to 19 murders, Gravano served less than four years and then entered WITSEC.

U.S. marshals sent Gravano and his family to Arizona, but instead of hiding out, he granted media interviews and collaborated with author Peter Maas on a book, *Underboss*, published in 1997. Relatives of his victims filed lawsuits totaling $25 million, but they never collected a cent. Meanwhile, Gravano returned to his old life of crime, selling illegal drugs with his son and members of a white-supremacist youth gang. Arrested in February 2000, Gravano was convicted in October 2002 and received a 19-year sentence. His son got nine years, while Gravano's wife and daughter—although charged—were not imprisoned. In February 2003 New Jersey prosecutors announced plans to try Gravano for a murder committed in 1980. At press time for this book, that case had not been tried.

killed him one block from the playground where his friend was slain in 2001. Explaining that lapse, Bronx Executive District Attorney Anthony Schepis told the *New York Times,* "You can't afford to put people up in a hotel and have armed guards for them in every case, because there just are not the resources."[14]

In 2005 San Francisco resident Nancy Burdell was sitting in a car parked near her home with her ex–boyfriend and their son. A gunman approached the vehicle and fired, killing the man and child. Burdell recognized the shooter and entered San Francisco County's witness-protection program to convict him. The killer was convicted and imprisoned, but Burdell still feels threatened. As she told National Public Radio in August 2007, "You basically feel like a caged animal. I feel my life is still in danger. I will always have to look over my shoulder." And that fear is well-founded. In 2006 another protected witness was gunned down in San Francisco after ignoring official warnings from the U.S. Marshals Service to stay out of town.[15]

WITSEC'S CRITICS

Since its creation in 1970, WITSEC has faced criticism on various fronts. One persistent complaint is the program's "coddling" of dangerous felons, including some guilty of numerous murders. One such subject, New York mobster Salvatore Gravano, convicted more than 50 fellow gangsters. In return, after confessing to 19 homicides, he spent only three and a half years in prison—less than three months per murder.[16]

Concealing criminals creates another problem when WITSEC subjects return to their old lives of crime. The Marshals Service says that only 17 percent of all protected witnesses have been arrested for new crimes while under WITSEC's cover; those crimes include at least 20 known murders.[17] Clearly, marshals cannot be responsible for every subject's actions, except when a witness is guarded around the clock, but such incidents still hurt the program's reputation.

Another complaint involves money. WITSEC subjects are required to settle all outstanding debts, including criminal fines and civil lawsuit obligations, before they receive new identities, but some are also permitted to keep fortunes accumulated during criminal activities. In one case, marshals moved drug dealer Floyd Canceres, 20 relatives, and a babysitter from Panama to a new home in the United States, at a cost of $211,681.[18]

Critics note that Congress has not reviewed WITSEC procedures since 1982, when hearings focused on the crimes of subject Marion Albert Pruett. Pruett was serving time in federal prison when he witnessed an inmate's murder and agreed to testify against the killer. He entered WITSEC in 1979 as "Charles Pearson," then went on a murder rampage that claimed at least five lives over the next two years. These murders spanned four states—Arkansas, Colorado, Mississippi, and New Mexico—and, when captured, Pruett also confessed to killing a cellmate in Georgia. Arkansas authorities executed Pruett in April 1999.[19]

Another disturbing case involved James Allen Red Dog, a Sioux Indian and career criminal serving time for four murders when he agreed to testify against his own accomplices in a slaying at the federal prison in Marion, Illinois. Both defendants were acquitted in 1987, while Red Dog was released into WITSEC and relocated to Delaware. In 1991 he bound and nearly beheaded a Wilmington man, then kidnapped and raped a female witness to the murder. She escaped and called police, resulting in Red Dog's arrest, conviction, and execution in February 1993.[20]

Periodic audits of WITSEC also cast doubt on claims concerning the behavior of protected witnesses. A report from 1983 says, "Auditors identified seven witnesses who have been convicted of murder, one who is currently charged with murder, and indications that four others were charged with murders. Other serious crimes committed by witnesses include arson, robbery and assorted drug violations." Nine years later, another audit found that one-fifth of all WITSEC subjects admitted since 1989 had committed new crimes, and noted, "Witness program officials refused to provide sufficient information for the study to be complete."[21]

Defense attorneys often claim that sheltered witnesses lie under oath, sometimes falsely blaming others for their own crimes. William Koopman, a mobster from Buffalo, New York, admitted involvement in seven murders and agreed to testify against former friends in return for a five-year prison term. Seven months after his release, in 1995, Koopman confessed to lying at one trial—blaming an innocent defendant for the murder of a victim shot by Koopman. Despite his WITSEC contract's provision for prosecution if Koopman committed perjury, he remains free today.[22]

Some WITSEC subjects also claim that they were tricked into joining the program and then denied protection or other promised services. George Taylor was imprisoned in Missouri for armed robbery and drug dealing when he entered WITSEC, offered freedom and a new life in return for testimony against other criminals. Marshals moved him to a federal lockup in Arizona, but on the day of his release, says Taylor, all that he received was "a plane ticket and $30." Worse yet, his relocation forced him to miss several Missouri parole hearings, prompting authorities there to jail him for another two years. Federal officials now depict Taylor as "a vengeful liar."[23]

Dangerous Duty

Tahlequah, Oklahoma

Oklahoma's Going Snake District was named for a Cherokee chief who survived the long march on the "Trail of Tears" from Georgia to Oklahoma in 1838. Despite the tribe's defeat, violence continued on the reservation in Indian Territory, fueled by poverty and despair.

The bloodiest incident in U.S. Marshals Service history began on February 13, 1872, when Cherokee gunman Ezekiel "Zeke" Proctor shot white mill owner Jim Kecterson in the head and murdered his wife—a Cherokee. Proctor surrendered to Sheriff Jack Wright, and a trial was scheduled for April 15. Strangely, Cherokee tribal authorities charged Proctor only with assault, ignoring the murder of his wife. Relatives of victim Mary Beck Kecterson wanted him hanged for his crime.

Expecting trouble, Deputy U.S. Marshals Jacob Owens and James Peavy led a 10-man posse to the Cherokee school that served as a courtroom. Unfortunately, the posse included three Beck family members—Jesse, William, and Samuel—and one of their in-laws, all heavily armed. Subsequent events are shrouded by confusion. Some observers claimed the posse tried to kill Zeke Proctor and that his supporters fired in self-defense. Marshals Service historians describe the "Going Snake Massacre" as an unprovoked ambush and slaughter of lawmen assigned to protect the courthouse.

Today, even the names and number of the dead remain in doubt. The Marshals Service Web site lists eight victims from the posse:

Deputy Owens; Special Deputies Jesse and Sam Beck, Jim Ward, and Riley Woods; plus undeputized posse members William Beck and George Selvidge.[1] A separate tally, published by members of the Beck family, lists 10 dead: defense attorney Mose Alberty; seven posse members (Jesse and Sam Beck, plus Owens, Hicks, Selvidge, Ward, and Woods); Zeke Proctor's brother, Johnson; and bystander Andy Palone.[2]

Court reconvened on April 16, and a Cherokee jury acquitted Zeke Proctor of assaulting Jim Kecterson. Federal prosecutors then indicted Proctor for murdering Deputy Marshal Owens, but the charge was dismissed in 1873, allowing Proctor to return home as a celebrated tribal hero.

IN THE LINE OF FIRE

Enforcing federal laws can be dangerous business. Since 1794, a total of 250 U.S. marshals and deputy marshals have died in the line of duty. Those cases include 210 murders, 27 accidental deaths, three deaths from illness, and one from "unidentified" causes.[3]

The Old West was particularly dangerous for U.S. marshals. Aside from organized gangs of outlaws like those led by Bill Doolin and the Lee brothers, marshals faced constant threats from hostile Indian tribesmen and anyone else who objected to being arrested for federal crimes.

On January 17, 1887, Deputy Marshals William Kelly, Mark Kuykendall, John Phillips, and Henry Smith arrested a teenage suspected rustler in Indian Territory and then camped near the site of present-day Stidham, Oklahoma. Deputy Phillips rode 20 miles to Eufala on personal business and returned to find his three companions murdered with an axe, their bodies stacked on the campfire. Phillips buried his friends and pursued their killer, eventually recapturing him. The defendant was convicted of murder on July 13 and hanged on October 7, 1887.[4]

Deputy Marshal Phillips survived another eight months on the job. On June 30, 1888, he and Deputy Marshal William Whitson tried to arrest two brothers who disrupted a dance in Muskogee. The drunken carousers drew pistols and fired at close range, striking Phillips in the

WILLIAM "BILL" DOOLIN (1858–96)

Bill Doolin was one of the Old West's most notorious outlaws, operating throughout Arkansas, Kansas, and Oklahoma in the 1890s. He launched his criminal career as a member of the Dalton Gang, led by bank-robbing brothers of Deputy U.S. Marshal Frank Dalton. A lame horse saved Doolin's life in October 1892 by causing him to miss a robbery in Coffeyville, Kansas, where townspeople gunned down the rest of his gang. Doolin then formed his own group, nicknamed "the Wild Bunch" (not to be confused with Butch Cassidy's Wild Bunch, based in Wyoming).

Doolin's bank and train holdups made him a high-priority target for U.S. marshals. The search focused on Ingalls, Oklahoma, after Doolin married a woman who lived there in March 1893. Five months later, on September 1, Doolin and six other Wild Bunch members gathered at a saloon in Ingalls. U.S. Marshal Evett Nix surrounded the bar with 13 deputies, and a ferocious battle erupted.

When the gun smoke cleared, Deputy Marshal Richard Speed was dead and Deputies Thomas Hueston and Lafayette Shadley were fatally wounded. A bystander, Young Simmons, was also killed while running for cover. Two other civilians were wounded, one after firing at the marshals. Of the seven bandits, only Roy Daugherty (alias "Arkansas Tom Jones") was captured, after being wounded. The rest escaped, although two—Dan "Dynamite Dick" Clifton and George "Bitter Creek" Newcomb—suffered bullet wounds. Townspeople threatened to lynch Daugherty, but marshals kept him alive to face trial.

Doolin eluded lawmen until August 1896. Traced to a hideout near Lawson, Oklahoma, Doolin made his last stand and was shot from his saddle by Deputy U.S. Marshal Heck Thomas. Over the next two years, the remaining Wild Bunch bandits died in shootouts with posses led by Oklahoma's "Three Guardsmen": Deputy Marshals Thomas, Chris Madsen, and Bill Tilghman.

head and killing him instantly. Deputy Whitson returned fire but suffered fatal wounds. The murderers escaped.[5]

On October 30, 1891, Deputy Marshal George Wise received word that whiskey smuggler Francisco Flores would be passing through Laredo, Texas, that night, with liquor imported from Mexico. Wise deputized two friends, Calixto Garcia and Fernando Salazar, to help him watch a house where Flores sometimes stayed. At 4:30 A.M. on October 31 Wise and his deputies saw Flores approaching the house. Wise confronted Flores with his pistol drawn and ordered him to halt. Flores laid down the bottles he was carrying and then rushed the lawmen with a dagger, fatally stabbing Wise and Garcia. Salazar, being unarmed, could not prevent the smuggler's escape back to Mexico.[6]

Less than six weeks later, Deputy Marshals Josiah Poorboy and Thomas Whitehead set out to arrest fugitive James Craig on the Cherokee Nation in Oklahoma. Before his escape, Craig had been arrested for adultery. His lover, the daughter of a Cherokee judge, hired three outlaws to ambush the marshals on December 8. After killing both marshals, the gunmen fled, but one—John Roach—was later killed by lawmen who arrested his accomplices, John Brown and Wacoo Hampton. Hampton testified against Brown, who was convicted of murder and sentenced to death in February 1892. Brown appealed his case and fought the charge in three more trials; he ended up spending only one year in a federal prison.[7]

On September 13, 1892, Deputy Marshals Andrew McGinnis and Vernon Wilson tried to arrest notorious train robbers Chris Evans and John Sontag, wanted for the recent murder of a California sheriff's deputy. They found the outlaws in Tulare County, and a shootout ensued, leaving both marshals dead. Sontag died in a later battle with authorities, while Evans was captured and sentenced to life in Folsom Prison. Governor Hiram Johnson paroled him in 1911.[8]

Even religious meetings could be dangerous. On July 17, 1898, Deputy Marshals Boley Grady and Bud Hill entered Pushmataha County, Oklahoma, to arrest Floyd Simpson for throwing eggs and rocks at a tent revival. When they confronted Simpson, he called to his father, William, for help. William Simpson killed Deputy Boley, while Floyd disarmed Hill and shot him with his own pistol. Hill lived long enough to identify the slayers, but William Simpson remained at large until 1904. Jurors acquitted both Simpsons at trial.[9]

Brothers Christopher and William Corbin, both deputy U.S. marshals, survived several gunfights in the early 1900s, but their luck ran

THE LEE GANG

The Lee Gang was a group of livestock rustlers led by brothers James, Pink, and Tom Lee. Their base of operations was a ranch in Cooke County, Texas, but they also ranged widely through Indian Territory (now Oklahoma), where James Lee had married a Chickasaw woman. Outlaws from all parts of Texas and Oklahoma used the Lee ranch as a hideout between robberies. They also sold liquor to Native American tribes, a federal crime in itself.

In late April 1885 rancher James Roff saw the Lees stealing some of his cattle and reported the theft to U.S. Marshal James Guy. Marshal Guy deputized Roff and his brother Andy, along with two others, Bill Kirksey and Frances Mathes. Together, on May 1, they followed the rustlers' trail to a point near Calico Creek, Oklahoma, where they found a fortified log cabin. As they approached the hideout, gunfire blazed from its windows, fatally wounding Marshal Guy, the Roff brothers, and Bill Kirksey. Only Deputy Mathes survived, and the outlaws escaped.

On May 3 a civilian mob raided and burned the Lee ranch. Two gang members, the Dyer brothers, were soon caught and lynched in Lamar, Oklahoma, while authorities offered a $7,000 reward for the Lees and brother-in-law Ed Steine. Deputy Marshal Heck Thomas tracked Jim and Pink Lee to a hideout near Lake Texoma, where both died in a shootout with the marshal's posse. Lawmen later caught Tom Lee and Ed Steine in Denison, Texas, shipping them off for trial at Fort Smith, Arkansas, where jurors acquitted both suspects. Steine returned to bootlegging, and ultimately drank himself to death. Tom Lee was finally convicted and imprisoned for larceny.

out on March 8, 1909, when they tried to arrest Robert Belcher outside Walhalla, South Carolina. Belcher was wanted for shooting up his grandmother's mailbox, yet he hid on her farm. The Corbins found him in the barn that night and were attempting to remove him when relatives killed both marshals with close-range gunfire. Belcher was later caught and received a 20-year sentence.[10]

MOONSHINE WARS

No job has proved more dangerous for U.S. marshals than pursuing violators of federal liquor laws. Between 1869 and 1935, 52 deputy marshals lost their lives to bootleggers and smugglers.[11] They include

- *Deputy Marshal Theodore Moses,* shot in his sleep on December 6, 1869, by a Missouri moonshiner whom he planned to arrest the next day.[12]
- *Deputy Marshal Maddison Mitchell,* ambushed and killed while escorting a bootlegger to jail in Pickens County, South Carolina, on June 18, 1872.[13]
- *Deputy Marshal George Ellis,* shot while trying to arrest a bootlegging suspect in Casey County, Kentucky, on December 10, 1877. Before collapsing, Ellis killed his attacker.[14]
- *Deputy Marshal Rufus Springs,* shot from ambush as he joined other marshals to raid a South Carolina whiskey still on April 19, 1878. The other officers fled.[15]
- *Special Deputy Marshal Jack Kimbrew,* shot while raiding a moonshine still in Hancock County, Georgia, on September 10, 1878. He died the following day.[16]
- *Deputy Marshal John Hardie,* killed by a shotgun blast while raiding a still in Marshall County, Alabama, on December 8, 1880. A second deputy was also wounded.[17]
- *Special Deputy Marshals Addison Beck and Lewis Merritt,* shot and killed while trying to arrest a liquor-violation suspect in Muskogee County, Oklahoma, on September 27, 1883.[18]
- *Deputy Marshal Walter Killion,* shot by a saloon owner in Lily, Kentucky, on May 24, 1884. The previous day, Killion had issued the barkeeper a citation for selling whiskey at illegally inflated prices.[19]

With a U.S. marshal standing watch at the bar, patrons gather at the Cosmopolitan Saloon in Telluride, Colorado, in this early-1900s photograph. Marshals kept a close eye on saloons for violations of liquor laws. *(Corbis)*

- *Deputy Marshal L. J. McDonald,* shot near Mitchellville, Tennessee, while trying to arrest a moonshiner on July 12, 1884.[20]
- *Deputy Marshal William Miller,* shot from ambush while searching for illegal stills in the mountains near Goodlettsville, Tennessee, on July 6, 1885.[21]
- *Deputy Marshal Miller Hurst,* ambushed near Jamestown, Tennessee, while transporting a moonshiner to jail in Nashville on October 11, 1888. The prisoner escaped and fled with the killers.[22]
- *Deputy Marshal Thomas Goodson,* killed on December 1, 1888, while trying to arrest illegal distillers in Carter County, Tennessee. His corpse was found near Roan Mountain on December 11.[23]

- *Deputy Marshal James Hager*, shot from ambush in Wyoming County, West Virginia, on August 10, 1889—one week after he was hired to track moonshiners in the county.[24]
- *Deputy Marshal Robert Cox*, shot in Claremore, Oklahoma, on April 14, 1890, by relatives of a man he arrested for selling whiskey at a barn dance.[25]
- *Deputy Marshal William Pitts*, killed with his own pistol after whiskey smugglers Jim Allen, Isam Frazier, and Lige Woods disarmed him at Lake West, Texas, on November 30, 1890. Frazier was imprisoned for manslaughter, and jurors acquitted Allen and Wood.[26]
- *Deputy Marshal Dan Osborne*, shot while trying to arrest a moonshiner in Cleburne County, Alabama, on November 20, 1891.[27]
- *Deputy Marshal Charles Stuart*, shot by bootleggers in eastern Tennessee on March 4, 1892.[28]
- *Deputy Marshal John Hamilton*, shot from ambush on April 23, 1892, in Owsley County, Kentucky, by four men he had earlier jailed for moonshining. Hamilton died on April 28.[29]
- *Deputy Marshal C. B. Brockus*, killed in a shootout with four moonshiners in Madison County, North Carolina, on February 16, 1893. Before he died, Brockus fatally wounded two outlaws. The others, Frank and John Lewellen, were acquitted of murder in May 1893.[30]
- *Special Deputy Marshal Calloway Garner*, shot on June 24, 1893, while raiding a bootlegger's home in Hardin County, Tennessee. Another marshal was also wounded.[31]
- *Special Deputy Marshal J. Perry Griggs*, killed while trying to arrest two moonshiners in Cherokee County, Georgia, on August 10, 1893.[32]
- *Deputy Marshal Thomas Martin*, shot on his front porch, on June 4, 1894, by Arkansas bootleggers whom he was investigating.[33]
- *Deputy Marshal M. W. Nix*, shot near Sallisaw, Oklahoma, as he approached the home of suspected moonshiners on August 3, 1894. Gunman William Ford surrendered and escaped charges, claiming that he thought Nix was a criminal. Investigators found that Nix approached the house with gun drawn, and did not identify himself.[34]

- *Deputy Marshal Thomas Grissom*, shot while trying to arrest a moonshiner in Pike County, Arkansas, on September 13, 1894. The killer was captured in January 1895.
- *Deputy Marshal Boyd Arnett*, gunned down while trying to arrest a bootlegger in White Oak, Kentucky, on August 20, 1895.[35]
- *Deputy Marshal Edward Thurlo*, shot while searching a wagonload of illegal whiskey in Duncan, Oklahoma, on February 10, 1896.[36]
- *Deputy Marshal John Kirby*, shot while raiding an illegal still near Holly Springs, South Carolina, on March 5, 1896. Two other marshals were wounded.[37]
- *Deputy Marshal Joseph Heinrichs*, shot on March 15, 1899, at his home in Tahlequah, Oklahoma, by a prisoner detained for selling whiskey on an Indian reservation. The suspect escaped, but was recaptured on March 17.[38]
- *Deputy Marshal Thomas Price*, shot during a raid on whiskey stills near Monterey, Tennessee, on July 20, 1901. Two local policemen were also wounded.[39]
- *Deputy Marshals John and Hugh Montgomery*, brothers, shot in Oxford, Mississippi, by two men suspected of bootlegging and counterfeiting, on November 17, 1901. The killers, also brothers, were hanged on September 24, 1902.[40]
- *Deputy Marshal J. N. Holsonback*, shot from ambush as he and his son escorted a moonshiner to jail near Boaz, Alabama, on January 11, 1902. Holsonback's son was also wounded. The prisoner was recaptured and received a 10-year sentence in October 1905.[41]
- *Deputy Marshal Edward Fink*, shot near Wetumka, Oklahoma, while trying to arrest two Indians caught with illegal whiskey on November 28, 1904. The gunman received a life sentence.[42]
- *Deputy Marshal Zack Wade*, shot by a suspected moonshiner near Rocky Mount, Virginia, on July 25, 1905. His slayer was convicted and hanged on November 24, 1905.[43]
- *Deputy Marshal George Williams*, slain while trying to arrest an Oklahoma whiskey smuggler on November 16, 1907. Another marshal shot and killed the gunman.[44]
- *Special Deputy Marshals Marion Ramey and John Sloan*, ambushed and shot in Dickenson County, Virginia, after demolishing an

illegal still on May 4, 1913. Ramey died instantly, while Sloan crawled five miles through the woods before dying. Two defendants were convicted and sentenced to life imprisonment.[45]

- *Deputy Marshals Holmes Davidson and William Plank*, gunned down in Tulsa, Oklahoma, on July 23, 1914, while serving a search warrant at the home of ex–police chief and convicted bootlegger William Baber. Baber claimed self-defense and stalled his trial until 1917, when he received a four-year sentence for manslaughter.[46]
- *Deputy Marshal C. P. Phelgar*, shot from ambush after raiding a still in Floyd County, Virginia, on May 14, 1915. Five suspects were jailed the next day.[47]
- *Deputy Marshal James Short*, murdered while serving a warrant to a moonshiner near Maulden, Kentucky, on May 26, 1923.[48]
- *Deputy Marshal Samuel Lilly*, killed on July 29, 1924, with Officer Leon George of the Wilmington, North Carolina, Police Department, while returning from a liquor raid. Bootleggers Charles Stewart and his son, William, were executed for the double murder on April 17, 1925.[49]
- *Deputy Marshal James Hill*, shot while searching the home of a suspected bootlegger in Seldovia, Alaska, on October 30, 1924.[50]
- *Deputy Marshal Adrian Metcalf*, shot in Harlan County, Kentucky, during a liquor raid on July 31, 1929. Other marshals wounded and captured the gunman, who had previously ambushed Metcalf and his sons in 1928.[51]
- *Deputy Marshal Reuben Hughett*, shot on June 13, 1930, while serving warrants on Prohibition violators in Knox County, Tennessee. Hughett died from his wounds on June 15.[52]
- *Deputy Marshal Clyde Rivers*, shot and killed when he and a deputy sheriff stopped a car driven by suspected bootleggers near Booneville, Mississippi, on May 16, 1931.[53]
- *Deputy Marshal W. F. Deiter*, struck on the head with a hammer during a liquor raid in San Juan, Puerto Rico, on February 26, 1932. His skull was fractured, and he died on March 1.[54]
- *Deputy Marshal Robert Sumter*, shot near Lehigh, Oklahoma, while serving court papers on August 9, 1933. Sumter was not engaged

in liquor raiding, but coincidentally found several men tending a moonshine still. The triggerman was convicted of murder and sentenced to 45 years in prison; he won parole in 1952.[55]

- *Deputy Marshal Herbert Ray*, killed in Lexington, Kentucky, while investigating reports of illegal liquor smuggling on February 2, 1935.[56]

Most Wanted

Perry, Florida

Business was slow at Daddy's Place, a barbershop in Perry, Florida, on May 25, 2009. It was Memorial Day, and most of the shop's regular customers were at home with their families, enjoying a day off from work. The barber had a single patron, 19-year-old Henry Hughes, when two other men entered the shop at 5:00 P.M.

The new arrivals drew guns and demanded money. Seconds later, shots rang out, killing Hughes and wounding the barber. Police identified the gunmen as 30-year-old Isaac Jackson III and 25-year-old Rufus Lee Jr. Both were members of the Bloods street gang, organized in Los Angeles during 1972 by enemies of the local Crips gang. Since then, both gangs had spread nationwide, leaving hundreds of corpses behind.

Police shared information on the Perry gunmen with the U.S. Marshals Florida Regional Fugitive Task Force. Five days after the shooting, on May 30, marshals found Jackson in Thomasville, Georgia, and placed him under arrest. Two days later, other task force members captured Lee in Fort Gaines, Georgia. On July 14 a Florida grand jury indicted both defendants for murder, attempted murder, and armed robbery. As an ex-convict, Lee faced added charges for possession of a firearm by a felon.

Florida's U.S. Marshal Dennis Williamson described the swift arrests as "yet another shining example of the extraordinary cooperation between the U.S. Marshals and state and local agencies to track down and capture dangerous fugitives who are wanted for violent offenses."[1]

HOT PURSUIT

Since 1789, U.S. marshals have been responsible for tracking and arresting federal fugitives. They were the national government's first manhunters (with a 76-year head start on the Secret Service, and a 119-year lead on the FBI). During its long, dramatic history, the Marshals Service has pursued some of America's most infamous felons, including the Dalton Gang, Bill Doolin's Wild Bunch, train robbers Chris Evans and John Sontag, and New Mexico's Billy the Kid.

And while most historians date the closing of the Wild West era at around 1900, pursuit of desperate criminals remains a daily fact of life for U.S. marshals. In 2008 marshals arrested more than 36,600 federal fugitives nationwide—more than the FBI, DEA, Secret Service, and all other federal law enforcement agencies combined. Aside from those arrests, marshals also participated in some 73,000 arrests of state and local fugitives, clearing a total of 90,600 felony warrants.[2]

The risks faced by U.S. marshals during fugitive investigations did not end with the taming of the West, as illustrated by five modern cases. In the first, on November 25, 1937, Deputy Marshal Raoul Dorsay and two plainclothes police officers entered an Oakland, California, apartment building, seeking a fugitive said to live there. The building's owner saw them with guns drawn, suspected they were criminals, and opened fire, killing Deputy Marshal Dorsay before the other officers identified themselves. No charges were filed.

On July 31, 1940, Marshal George Meffan and Deputy Marshal John Glenn went to arrest a squatter at his illegal residence on federal property north of Boise, Idaho. The subject, Pearl Royal Hendrickson, had been ordered to leave and faced charges for contempt of court. Unwilling to vacate his cabin, Hendrickson had warned Forest Service employees, "If they come after me, they better bring an undertaker."[3] When the two marshals arrived, Hendrickson shot and killed both of them, sparking a three-hour siege during which 50 officers riddled his cabin with bullets and set it afire with dynamite charges. Hendrickson

BILLY THE KID

Henry McCarty was known by several names during his short and violent life. Historians still argue over the name he received at birth, in November 1859, with various authors claiming it was Edward, Michael, Patrick, or William. "Henry" remains the most popular choice—perhaps because McCarty used it with another alias, "Henry Antrim." Then again, he also called himself "William Bonney"—but most Americans know him as "Billy the Kid."

Born to Irish immigrant parents in New York City, McCarty moved to Indiana with his mother and a younger brother at age nine. Five years later, with a new stepfather, the family settled in New Mexico. Henry's mother died in 1874, and his stepfather vanished, abandoning the youth to live with neighbors who could not control him. His first arrest, in April 1875, involved a theft of cheese. Five months later he was caught with clothes and firearms stolen from a Chinese laundry. McCarty escaped after two days in jail. He spent the rest of his life as a fugitive from justice.

Rustling livestock was Billy the Kid's primary occupation, but he also honed his gunfighting skills, killing his first known

was wounded and dying by the time police dragged him from the flaming wreckage.

In another incident, Deputy Marshal Henry Dale was searching for a fugitive in Chicago, Illinois, when he accidentally interrupted a liquor store robbery on July 14, 1971. The four bandits turned their guns on Dale, fatally wounding him, but Dale killed one of the bandits before the other three escaped. Those fugitives were caught a few days later, convicted of murder and robbery.

Political extremist Gordon Kahl wrote a letter to the Internal Revenue Service in 1967, announcing that he would no longer pay income taxes. Prosecutors waited nine years to charge him with tax evasion, opponent in 1877. Some authors credit Billy with killing one man for each year of his life, while others cite lower figures—as few as four victims, by one account.[4] He is remembered today for his role in New Mexico's Lincoln County War, which claimed 22 lives between February and July 1878.[5]

That feud prompted McCarty to kill four lawmen. On April 1, 1878, he shot Sheriff William Brady and Deputy George Hindman in Lincoln, blaming them for the death of a friend slain in custody two months earlier. Captured in December 1880 and charged with murder, McCarty escaped from Lincoln's jail on April 28, 1881, killing Deputy U.S. Marshal Robert Olinger and Deputy Sheriff James Bell in the process.

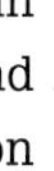

The task of hunting Billy the Kid then fell to Patrick Garrett, who served both as Lincoln County's sheriff and as a deputy U.S. marshal. While some authors claim Garrett was a longtime friend of Billy's, no evidence supports that story. Garrett tracked McCarty to a girlfriend's home in Fort Sumner and killed him there on July 14, 1881. Unproven claims persist, encouraged by Hollywood films, that Billy faked the incident with Garrett's help and lived to a ripe old age in retirement. Garrett was killed by a neighbor in a dispute over grazing land on February 29, 1908.

and Kahl served a year in prison. On February 13, 1983, U.S. marshals sought to arrest Kahl for felony parole violations at his Nebraska ranch. Kahl, his son, and two friends opened fire with automatic weapons, killing Deputy Marshals Robert Cheshire Jr. and Kenneth Muir. The shootout also killed Kahl's son and left his friends facing life prison terms, while Kahl escaped in a stolen police car. On June 3, 1983, U.S. marshals and local police traced Kahl to a friend's home near Smithville, Arkansas. Another battle erupted, during which Kahl murdered Lawrence County Sheriff Gene Matthews and then died as fire swept through his hideout. Kahl remains a hero to neo-Nazi groups that despise the federal government.

Another extremist, Idaho Aryan Nations associate Randall Weaver, sold an illegal sawed-off shotgun to ATF agents in January 1991 and then failed to appear for a court date in February. Apparently, a careless court clerk sent Weaver a notice placing the hearing in March, a month after its actual date. Charged with firearms violations and failure to appear, Weaver became a federal fugitive. U.S. marshals sought to arrest him on August 21, 1992, at Weaver's remote mountain cabin, but they walked into an ambush by Weaver's son and family friend Kevin Harris. The shootout killed Deputy Marshal William Degan Jr. and Weaver's son. FBI agents then surrounded Weaver's home for a 10-day siege that also left Weaver's wife dead. At his trial for murder and other crimes, jurors acquitted Weaver of all counts except failure to appear, for which he received an 18-month sentence and a $10,000 fine. Gunman Kevin Harris was also cleared of Degan's murder, on a plea of self-defense. Weaver sued the government over his wife's death, receiving a $380,000 settlement in September 2000.

WORST OF THE WORST

FBI Director J. Edgar Hoover scored a publicity coup in March 1950 when he created the bureau's "Ten Most Wanted Fugitives" program, coordinating publicity with newspapers, TV networks, and other media outlets worldwide. By October 21, 2009, 463 out of 494 "Top 10" FBI fugitives had been captured, 152 of them through tips from civilians alerted by media publicity.[6] The "most wanted" concept caught on with other federal, state, and local agencies—and in the media itself, with programs such as *America's Most Wanted.*

The U.S. Marshals Service created its own 15 Most Wanted Fugitive Program in 1983, as explained by agency spokesmen, "To prioritize the investigation and apprehension of high-profile offenders who are considered to be some of the country's most dangerous fugitives."[7] Top 15 fugitives tend to be career criminals with histories of violence—murderers, sexual predators, drug kingpins, members of organized crime, and so on—whose offenses pose a serious threat to public safety.

Unlike the FBI, the Marshals Service does not publish running tallies of "most wanted" fugitive arrests. The agency's Web site does offer a sampling of 42 listed felons, captured between May 2003 and November

2008, but with no suggestion of how many others were caught.[8] Those still at large as this book went to press include

- *Raymond Abbott,* an illegal arms dealer sought for escape from a federal lockup in Puerto Rico.
- *Larry Chism,* a convicted armed robber, kidnapper, and airline hijacker, who escaped from custody in 1978.
- *David Creamer,* a child pornographer and money launderer, once arrested with 70 guns and 80,000 rounds of ammunition.
- *Paul Eischeid,* a member of the Hells Angels motorcycle gang, sought for drug trafficking and stabbing a woman to death.
- *Joseph Garcia,* a contract killer for the Mexican Mafia prison gang and Mexican drug cartels.
- *Daniel Hiers,* wanted on charges of killing his wife and molesting multiple children.
- *Robert King,* a Tennessee fugitive sought for killing his girlfriend and attempting to kill her mother.
- *Frederick McLean,* a serial child molester with crimes spanning 25 years.
- *Andre Neverson,* a native of Trinidad, deported in 2000 after serving five years for attempted murder, who returned to the United States illegally and killed two victims—his sister and fiancée—in July 2002.
- *John Ruffo,* a corporate criminal who defrauded various banks of $350 million, then fled while appealing his conviction.
- *Vincent Walters,* a California murder suspect.
- *Randy Yager,* a member of the Outlaws motorcycle gang, charged with multiple murders, plus arson, counterfeiting, explosives, firearms, and narcotics charges.

The list's final three slots were empty at press time due to arrests.

MAJOR CASES

The Marshals Service created its Major Case Fugitive Program in 1985 to supplement the already successful 15 Most Wanted list. Criteria for classification as a major case are similar to those for the Top 15 program, targeting "offenders who are considered to be some of the country's most dangerous individuals."[9] At press time for this book, the Major Case list included 48 fugitives, some of whom may be elevated to "most wanted" status as members of the Top 15 list are arrested.[10]

Twenty-five of the current 48 major case fugitives are charged with drug offenses. Two are charged with homicide, one with extortion, one with racketeering, one with rape, and one with child molestation. The others face charges of escape, failure to appear for trial on various charges, and probation violation.[11]

Pursuit of fugitives often involves cooperation between different law enforcement agencies. At present, the U.S. Marshals Service is the lead agency for 91 interagency fugitive task forces, which include officers from various federal, state, and local agencies.[12] These task forces are aided by the Marshals Service's Technical Operations Group, and by its Criminal Information Branch, which performs research and analysis related to fugitive investigations. The Marshals Service is also designated by the Department of Justice as the primary agency responsible for apprehending foreign fugitives at large in the United States, for delivery to officers of their native countries.

FALCON'S WINGS

In April 2005, as part of National Crime Victims' Rights Week, the U.S. Marshals Service joined 958 other federal, state, and local law enforcement agencies to carry out Operation FALCON (*F*ederal *a*nd *L*ocal *C*ops *O*rganized *N*ationally). The sweep for fugitives was carried out in all 50 states, plus Puerto Rico and Guam. Between April 4 and 10, it bagged more prisoners than any other single police operation in history.[13]

The final haul for Operation FALCON included 10,340 fugitives named in 13,851 felony warrants. Seventy-one percent of those arrested had served time on prior convictions for crimes of violence. The new cases included 144 fugitives accused or convicted of murder, 553 charged with rape or sexual assault, 638 wanted for armed robbery, 4,291 sought for narcotics violations, 1,818 charged with burglary, 1,727 wanted for assault, and 154 gang members. Aside from prisoners, officers involved in Operation FALCON seized 243 weapons, 66

PAUL HERMAN CLOUSTON

Detective Darrel Cate was assigned to the Buena Park (California) Police Department's Crimes-Against-Persons Unit in September 1972, when his dispatcher received a complaint of sexual assault. The victim, a pregnant housewife, identified her attacker as Paul Drago, living at 939 Emerald Street in nearby Anaheim. Cate and his partner, Detective Dale Willson, drove to that address on September 21 and found a man outside, working underneath a jacked-up car.

The man identified himself as Herman Clouston, said he lived at 931 Emerald, and claimed he was repairing the car for a friend. Detective Willson walked to the second house, seeking to verify Clouston's story, while Detective Cate followed Clouston into 939 Emerald, allegedly to retrieve an I.D. card. Instead, Clouston grabbed a pistol and shot Cate twice, inflicting wounds that claimed his life an hour later.

Investigators soon identified the gunman as Paul Herman Clouston, a Pennsylvania native born in 1935. His criminal record dated from 1954 and included convictions in West Virginia and Ohio for auto theft, burglary, larceny, and escape. He was a fugitive from a 1966 Ohio prison break when he killed Detective Cate. Before his arrest on September 27, Clouston broke into another home and kidnapped its occupant. On August 1, 1973, jurors convicted him of second-degree murder, burglary, and kidnapping. Sentenced to three concurrent 10-year terms, he was released in January 1982.[14]

He remained a menace to society. In 1991 he was imprisoned on 17 counts of molesting children in Williamsburg, Virginia. Paroled again in 2005, he failed to register as a convicted sex offender and fled into hiding. Wanted in Virginia for parole violation and failure to register (a separate crime in itself), Clouston was arrested on June 2, 2010. The U.S. Marshals Service had added his name to its 15 Most Wanted list on November 30, 2006, offering a $25,000 reward for information leading to his arrest.[15]

pounds of of cocaine, 42 pounds of heroin, 449 pounds of marijuana, and $373,000 in cash.[16]

Operation FALCON proved so successful that it was repeated in April 2006, again in conjunction with National Crime Victims' Rights Week. Operation FALCON II involved members of 793 law enforcement agencies, including six foreign police departments. Between April 17 and 23, raiders striking throughout the United States, Guam, and the Northern Mariana Islands captured 9,037 fugitives and cleared 10,419 felony warrants. Those arrested included 73 murder suspects, 462 fugitives charged with violent sex crimes, 311 wanted for other sex crimes, 783 convicted sex offenders who failed to register as required by law, and 163 documented gang members. FALCON II also recovered 111 guns, 200 pounds of illegal drugs, 14 vehicles, and $120,265 in cash.[17]

Operation FALCON III was executed in October 2006 and was restricted in scope to 24 states east of the Mississippi River. Officers from 1,045 different law enforcement agencies, all deputized as special deputy U.S. marshals, arrested 10,733 fugitives from justice, clearing 13,333 outstanding felony warrants. Those jailed between October 22 and 28 included 107 murder suspects, 1,659 sex offenders, 364 documented gang members, and others sought on a range of charges, including burglary, carjacking, kidnapping, robbery, and weapons violations. A total of 3,451 fugitives were caught with illegal drugs and thus faced additional charges beyond their existing warrants. Officers involved in FALCON III also seized 455 weapons and 164 vehicles.[18]

Operation FALCON 2007 was a more protracted campaign, involving officers from 540 federal, state, and local law enforcement agencies. The program was launched with Operation FALCON-Baltimore in February, targeting street gangs and jailing 195 fugitives. Operation FALCON-Indianapolis followed in May 2007, producing 283 arrests. Between June and September, local FALCON campaigns in 27 more U.S. cities bagged 6,406 fugitives and cleared 7,766 felony warrants. Those arrested included 73 homicide suspects, 566 sex offenders, 19 arsonists, 882 burglars, 31 kidnappers, 2,227 narcotics dealers, 342 members of organized crime, and 300 documented gang members. The sweep also captured 249 firearms.[19]

U.S. marshals and a Tennessee Bureau of Investigation agent participate in the fugitive roundup code-named Operation Falcon III in Sevierville, Tennessee, in October 2006. *(AP Photo/*Knoxville News Sentinel*, Joe Howell)*

Operation FALCON 2008 returned to the program's original roots as a nationwide campaign to apprehend fugitives. Between June 15 and 21, officers from 1,627 law enforcement agencies arrested 19,380 fugitives from coast to coast, clearing 25,087 felony warrants. Collectively, those captured in the sweep had nearly 94,000 prior arrests. The group included 161 murder suspects, 1,096 sex offenders, 6,252 narcotics violators, 796 persons wanted for federal weapons violations, and 388 documented gang members. Aside from those arrested, officers involved in Operation FALCON 2008 seized 418 weapons, 34 vehicles, more than 5,280 pounds of illegal drugs, and $1.5 million in cash.[20]

The latest FALCON operation, carried out in June 2009, broke all records set by previous campaigns. Over the span of four weeks, officers representing 2,224 law enforcement agencies arrested 35,190 fugitives from justice nationwide, clearing 47,418 outstanding felony warrants. Those arrested had police records revealing a total of 138,220 prior arrests. They included 433 murder suspects, 2,356 sex offenders, 10,525 persons charged with drug crimes, 1,677 wanted on federal weapons charges, and 900 documented gang members. In addition to fugitives captured, FALCON 2009 raiders seized 582 guns, 38 vehicles, some 5,200 pounds of narcotics, and $342,179 in cash.[21]

Chronology

1789	**September 24**: President George Washington appoints the first 13 U.S. marshals
1794	**January 11**: Robert Forsyth becomes the first U.S. marshal killed on duty
	August–October: Pennsylvania's Whiskey Rebellion
1798	**July 13:** The Sedition Act turns marshals into reluctant censors
1850	**September 18:** Congress passes the Fugitive Slave Act
1862	**July 29:** Marshal Keyes arrests Confederate spy Belle Boyd
1870	**July 1:** Department of Justice created
1872	**April 15:** Eight marshals and 14 Cherokees die in an Oklahoma shootout
1881	**July 14:** Marshal Pat Garrett kills Billy the Kid in New Mexico
	October 26: O.K. Corral gunfight in Tombstone, Arizona
1883	**September 27:** Outlaws kill two marshals in Indian Territory
1885	**May 1:** The Lee Gang kills three marshals in a Texas ambush
1887	**January 17:** Three marshals murdered by a prisoner near Eufala, Oklahoma
1888	**June 30:** Two marshals die in a shootout with an Oklahoma gunman
1890	**April 14:** The Supreme Court confirms police powers of U.S. marshals

1891	**December 8:** Cherokee assassins murder two marshals in Oklahoma
1892	**September 13:** California train robbers kill two marshals
	November 3: Marshals kill Arkansas outlaw Ned Christie, ending a four-year siege
1893	**September 1:** Three marshals fatally wounded in battle with the Doolin Gang
1894	**May:** Marshals and U.S. troops crush the Pullman Strike in Illinois
1896	**August 24:** Marshal Heck Thomas kills outlaw Bill Doolin in Oklahoma
1897	**August 29:** Moonshiners kill two marshals in Arkansas
1898	**July 17:** A religious fanatic kills two marshals in Oklahoma
1901	**November 17:** A Mississippi bootlegger kills two marshals
1909	**March 8:** A mailbox vandal kills two marshals in South Carolina
1913	**May 4:** Kentucky moonshiners kill two marshals
1914	**July 23:** An ex–police chief kills two marshals in Tulsa, Oklahoma
1920	**January 16:** The Eighteenth Amendment bans alcoholic beverages
1927	**April 1:** The Department of the Treasury's Prohibition Bureau relieves the U.S. Marshals Service of liquor enforcement
1940	**July 31:** A man sought for contempt of court kills two marshals in Idaho
1954	**May 17:** The Supreme Court orders integration of public schools
1956	**December17:** Executive Office of U.S. Marshals created
1960	**November 14:** Marshals escort Ruby Bridges Hall to a newly integrated New Orleans school

1961	**May 21:** Marshals guard freedom riders in Montgomery, Alabama
1962	**September 30:** Marshals battle racist rioters at the University of Mississippi
1967	**October 21:** Marshals confront antiwar protesters at the Pentagon
1970	**October 15:** Federal Witness Security Program created
1971	**January:** Special Operations Group (SOG) created
	May 3: SOG deployed for antiwar protests in Washington, D.C.
1973	**February 27–May 5:** Siege at Wounded Knee, South Dakota
1979	National Prisoner Transportation System created
	October: Marshals assume responsibility for apprehending federal fugitives
1981	**October 1:** First Fugitive Investigative Strike Team organized in Florida
1982	**December 3:** Court Security Officer program established
1983	**February 13:** Tax evader Gordon Kahl kills two marshals in North Dakota
1984	**October 12:** Comprehensive Crime Control Act creates Asset Forfeiture Program
1987	**November 21–December 4:** SOG marshals contain federal prison riots in Georgia and Louisiana
1989	**September 25:** SOG marshals deployed in U.S. Virgin Islands after Hurricane Hugo
1989–1990	**April 1989–February 1990:** Pittson coal strike in West Virginia
1990	**January 3:** SOG marshals transport Manuel Noriega from Panama to the United States
1992	**February 18–April 30:** Operation Gunsmoke captures 3,300 fugitives
	April 29–May 4: SOG marshals patrol Los Angeles riot zone

	July 20: A prisoner kills two marshals and himself in Chicago's federal courthouse
	August 21–September 1: Randy Weaver siege at Ruby Ridge, Idaho
	October 13–November 24: Operation Gunsmoke II bags 1,078 fugitives
1993	**Summer:** Operation Trident captures 5,788 fugitives in 58 cities
1995	**October 1:** Justice Prisoner and Alien Transportation System begins operation
1998	**March:** Theatrical release of *U.S. Marshals*, starring Tommy Lee Jones
2000	**May 4–9:** SOG marshals remove protesters from a U.S. Navy base in Puerto Rico
2005	**April 4–10:** Operation Falcon captures 10,340 fugitives
2006	**April 17–23**: Operation Falcon II nets 9,037 fugitives
	July: Fugitive Safe Surrender program inaugurated
	October 22–28: Operation Falcon III captures 10,733 fugitives
2007	**June–September:** Operation Falcon 2007 bags 6,406 fugitives
2008	**June:** Operation Falcon 2008 captures 19,380 fugitives
2009	**April:** Deputy Marshal John Ambrose convicted of leaking WITSEC information

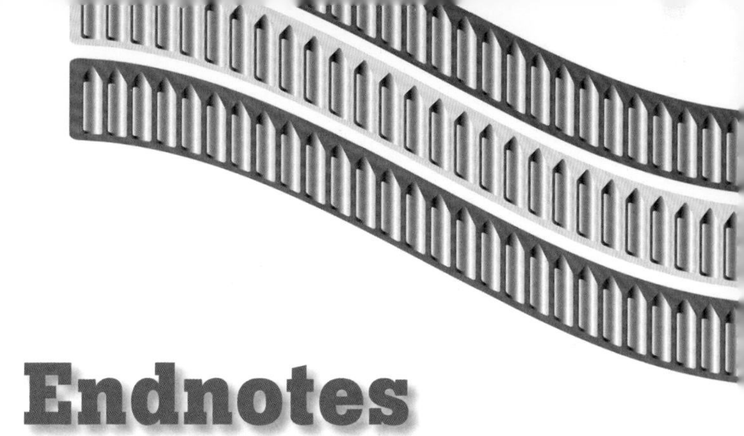

Endnotes

Introduction

1. Bureau of Justice Statistics, "Law Enforcement," http://bjs.ojp.usdoj.gov/index.cfm?ty=tp&tid=7 (Accessed August 13, 2010).
2. U.S. Marshals Service, "General Information," http://www.justice.gov/marshals/duties/factsheets/general-1209.html (Accessed August 13, 2010).
3. Ibid.

Chapter 1

1. Officer Down Memorial Page, "Special Deputy Marshal Harry A. Belluomini," http://www.odmp.org/officer/358-deputy-marshal-harry-a.-belluomini (Accessed August 13, 2010).
2. Steve Warmbir, "Man gets 20 years for lying about role in escape," *Chicago Sun-Times,* September 13, 2002.
3. *United States of America v. Robert A. Burke,* http://207.41.16.133/rfcViewFile/09cv2107motion.pdf (Accessed August 20, 2010).
4. U.S. Marshals Service, "Witness Security Program," http://www.usmarshals.gov/witsec/americas_star.pdf (Accessed August 13, 2010).
5. U.S. Marshals Service, "Fact Sheets," http://www.usmarshals.gov/duties/factsheets/facts-1209.html (Accessed August 13, 2010).
6. U.S. Marshals Service, "Nomination Process for U.S. Marshals," http://www.usmarshals.gov/oca/nominations.pdf (Accessed August 13, 2010).
7. U.S. Marshals Service, "Judicial Security," http://www.justice.gov/marshals/judicial (Accessed August 13, 2010).
8. Ibid.
9. Ibid.
10. U.S Marshals Service, "Justice Prisoner & Alien Transportation System," http://www.usmarshals.gov/jpats/index.html (Accessed August 13, 2010).
11. U.S Marshals Service, "Witness Security Program," http://www.usmarshals.gov/witsec/index.html (Accessed August 13, 2010).
12. U.S Marshals Service, "Fugitive Investigations," http://www.usmarshals.gov/investigations/index.html (Accessed August 13, 2010).
13. Ibid.
14. "The Shadow Stalkers," http://www.militaryphotos.net/forums/showthread.php?t=7835-US-Marshals-Service-SOG (Accessed August 13, 2010).
15. U.S. Marshals Service, "Tactical Operations," http://www.

usmarshals.gov/duties/ops.htm (Accessed August 13, 2010).
16. Robert D. McFadden, "Cubans in 2d jail riot over fears of deportation," *New York Times*, November 24, 1987.
17. "The Shadow Stalkers."
18. U.S. Marshals Service, "Operation Falcon," http://www.usmarshals.gov/falcon09/news_releases/national_release.htm (Accessed August 13, 2010).
19. U.S. Marshals Service, "Fugitive Investigations," http://www.justice.gov/marshals/investigations/index.html (Accessed August 13, 2010).

Chapter 2

1. Officer Down Memorial Page, "United States Department of Justice—Marshals Service," http://www.odmp.org/agency/3955-united-states-department-of-justice---marshals-service-u.s.-government (Accessed August 13, 2010).
2. Constitution of the United States of America, Article III, Section 1.
3. Judiciary Act of 1789 (1 Stat. 73-93).
4. U.S. Marshals Service, "History—The First Generation of United States Marshals," http://www.usmarshals.gov/history/firstmarshals/marshals1.htm (Accessed August 13, 2010).
5. Ibid.
6. Ibid.
7. Ibid.
8. Bill O'Neal, *The Pimlico Encyclopedia of Western Gunfighters* (London: Pimlico, 1998), 134–139.
9. Joseph Geringer, "Wyatt Earp's Legacy," TruTV, http://www.trutv.com/library/crime/gangsters_outlaws/outlaws/earp/1.html (Accessed September 1, 2010).
10. Ibid.
11. Ibid.
12. "Orrin Porter Rockwell," Utah History Encyclopedia, http://www.media.utah.edu/UHE/r/ROCKWELL,ORIN.html (Accessed August 13, 2010).
13. Richard Bushman, *Joseph Smith* (New York: Knopf, 2005), 468.
14. Stewart Durham, *The Smithsonian Guide to Historic America* (New York: Stewart, Tabori & Chang, 1990), 331–332.
15. Shawn Landis, "Orrin Porter Rockwell—Mormonism's Avenging Angel," suite101.com, http://www.suite101.com/content/orrin-porter-rockwell-a29711 (Accessed August 13, 2010).

Chapter 3

1. United States Census Bureau, "Fact Sheet," http://factfinder.census.gov/servlet/SAFFFacts?_event=Search&geo_id=&_geoContext=&_street=&_county=chesterfield&_cityTown=chesterfield&_state=04000US33&_zip=&_lang=en&_sse=on&pctxt=fph&pgsl=010&show_2003_tab=&redirect=Y (Accessed August 13, 2010).
2. "Fake Compaq products seized from reseller," ComputerWeekly.com, http://www.computerweekly.com/Articles/2002/02/15/185249/fake-compaq-products-seized-from-reseller.htm (Accessed August 13, 2010).
3. "Weare man sentenced," *Portsmouth* (N.H.) *Herald*, April 4, 2007.
4. "Raids by Microsoft uncover caches of counterfeit software," *New York Times*, October 8, 1992.

5. "BSA announces: Phoenix manufacturing company pays $135,000 to software watchdog; Raid reveals unlicensed software," http://www.thefreelibrary.com/BSA+Announces:+Phoenix+Manufacturing+Company+Pays+$135,000+to...-a068019869 (Accessed August 13, 2010).
6. Robert Blincoe, "U.S. marshals seize $1m fake Adaptec SCSI cards," *The Register*, http://www.theregister.co.uk/2000/10/31/us_marshals_seize_1m_fake/ (Accessed August 13, 2010).
7. RIAA Anti-Piracy Seizure Information, http://www.grayzone.com/april2002busts.htm (Accessed August 13, 2010).
8. "Man accused of impersonating marshal arrested in New York," WMUR-TV, Channel 9 (Manchester, N.H.), May 14, 2009.
9. The Proceedings of the Old Bailey, http://www.oldbaileyonline.org/browse.jsp?div=t16901015-36 (Accessed August 13, 2010).
10. Farley Grubb, "The Continental Dollar: How much was really issued?" *Journal of Economic History* 68 (March 2008), 283–291.
11. The History of U.S. Paper Money, http://www.ronscurrency.com/rhist.htm (Accessed August 13, 2010).
12. Arthur Nussbaum, "The law of the dollar," *Columbia Law Review* 7 (November 1937), 1057–1091.
13. U.S. Marshals Service, "History—Catching Counterfeiters," http://www.usmarshals.gov/history/counterfeit/counterfeit.htm (Accessed August 13, 2010).
14. Ibid.
15. Ibid.
16. Priscilla Rhoades, "King of the Confederate Counterfeit," *Kudzu Monthly*, http://www.kudzumonthly.com/kudzu/sep02/Kingof.html (Accessed August 13, 2010).
17. Ibid.
18. Ibid.
19. The History of U.S. Paper Money, http://www.ronscurrency.com/rhist.htm (Accessed August 13, 2010).
20. Thomas Craughwell, *Stealing Lincoln's Body* (Cambridge, Mass.: Belknap Press of Harvard University Press, 2007), 41–42.
21. Ibid., 42.
22. David Johnson, *Illegal Tender: Counterfeiting and the Secret Service in Nineteenth-Century America* (Washington D.C.: Smithsonian Institution Press, 1995), 76.
23. Officer Down Memorial Page, "Deputy Marshal Maston Reynolds (Boss) Greene," http://www.odmp.org/officer/5713-deputy-marshal-maston-reynolds-(boss)-greene (Accessed August 13, 2010).

Chapter 4

1. Matt Truell, "Topeka shooting," Associated Press, August 5, 1993.
2. U.S. Marshals Service, "Judicial Security," http://www.usmarshals.gov/judicial/index.html (Accessed August 13, 2010).
3. Ibid.
4. Ibid.
5. Ibid.
6. Ibid.
7. Ibid.
8. ADT Security Services, http://www.adt.com (Accessed August 13, 2010).
9. Ibid.

10. U.S. Marshals Service, "Defendants in Custody and Prisoner Management," http://www.usmarshals.gov/prisoner/index.html (Accessed August 13, 2010).
11. U.S. Marshals Service, "Justice Prisoner & Alien Transportation System," http://www.usmarshals.gov/jpats/index.html (Accessed August 13, 2010).
12. Ibid.
13. U.S. Marshals Service, "Asset Forfeiture Program," http://www.usmarshals.gov/assets/index.html (Accessed August 13, 2010).
14. Ibid.
15. Gary Tuchman and Katherine Wojtecki, "Texas police shake down drivers, lawsuit claims," CNN News, May 5, 2009.

Chapter 5

1. Officer Down Memorial Page, "Deputy Marshal James Batchelder," http://www.odmp.org/officer/1574-deputy-marshal-james-batchelder (Accessed August 13, 2010).
2. U.S. Marshals Service, "History," http://www.usmarshals.gov/history/index.html.
3. Ibid.
4. An Act Concerning Aliens; ch. 58, 1 Stat. 570.
5. An Act for the Punishment of Certain Crimes against the United States; ch. 74, 1 Stat. 596.
6. Officer Down Memorial Page.
7. William Helmer and Rick Mattix, *Public Enemies* (New York: Checkmark Books, 1998), 70.
8. Ibid., 65.
9. Old West Legends, "Bass Reeves," http://www.legendsofamerica.com/WE-BassReeves.html (Accessed August 13, 2010).
10. Ibid.
11. U.S. Marshals Service, "History—U.S. Marshals Role During Prohibition," http://www.usmarshals.gov/history/prohibition/index.html (Accessed August 13, 2010); Officer Down Memorial Page.
12. Taylor Branch, *Parting the Waters* (New York: Touchstone Books, 1988), 444–450.
13. Ibid., 454–465.
14. Gary May, *The Informant* (New Haven, Conn.: Yale University Press, 2005), 364.
15. Espionage Act, ch. 30, title I, 40 Stat. 219.
16. Amendment of May 16, 1918, ch. 75, 40 Stat. 553-54.
17. Espionage Act (1917) and Sedition Act (1918), Answers.com, http://www.answers.com/topic/espionage-act-1917-and-sedition-act-1918 (Accessed August 13, 2010).
18. William Doyle, *An American Insurrection* (New York: Anchor Books, 2001), 187.
19. Ibid., 280–281, 298; Michael Newton, *The Ku Klux Klan* (Jefferson, N.C.: McFarland, 2007), 300–302.
20. Scott Anderson, "The Martyrdom of Leonard Peltier," *Outside Magazine,* http://outsideonline.com/magazine/0795/7f_leo1.html (Accessed August 13, 2010).
21. Neely Tucker, "The wreckage of a dream," *Washington Post,* August 24, 2004.

Chapter 6

1. Thomas Farish, *History of Arizona* Vol. IV (San Francisco: Filmer Brothers, 1918), 137–138.
2. Eugene Wait, *America and the War of 1812* (Commack, N.Y.: Kroshka Books, 1999), 113.

3. "The Battle of New Orleans," NPS Historical Handbook: Jean Lafitte, http://www.nps.gov/history/history/online_books/hh/29/hh29m.htm (Accessed August 13, 2010).
4. Clint Tilton, "Lincoln and Lamon," *Publication of the Illinois State Historical Library* (1931), 189.
5. Norma Cuthbert, *Lincoln and the Baltimore Plot, 1861* (San Marino, Calif.: Huntington Library, 1949), 86.
6. Ward Lamon, *Life of Abraham Lincoln* (Boston: James R. Osgood, 1872), 513.
7. Officer Down Memorial Page, "Deputy Marshal R.T. Dunn," http://www.odmp.org/officer/4383-deputy-marshal-r.-t.-dunn (Accessed August 13, 2010).
8. Officer Down Memorial Page, "Deputy Marshal James P. Everette," http://www.odmp.org/officer/4687-deputy-marshal-james-p.-everette (Accessed August 13, 2010).
9. U.S. Marshals Service, "History—The U.S. Marshals during World War I," http://www.usmarshals.gov/history/ww1/ww1.htm (Accessed August 13, 2010).
10. "Italian American Internment," NationMaster, http://www.nationmaster.com/encyclopedia/Italian-American-internment (Accessed August 13, 2010).
11. Arthur Jacobs, "Internment of German Americans in the United States during World War II," http://www.foitimes.com (Accessed August 13, 2010).
12. Ibid.; "Italian American Internment," http://www.nationmaster.com/encyclopedia/Italian-American-internment (Accessed August 13, 2010); Ricco Siasoco and Shmuel Ross, "Japanese Relocation Centers," http://www.infoplease.com/spot/internment1.html (Accessed August 13, 2010).
13. U.S. Marshals Service, "History—U.S. Marshals and the Pentagon Riot of October 21, 1967," http://www.usmarshals.gov/history/civilian/1967a.htm (Accessed August 13, 2010).
14. Ibid.
15. U.S. Marshals Service, "History—Anti-war Demonstrations: The Gulf War," http://www.usmarshals.gov/history/civilian/gulf_war.htm (Accessed August 13, 2010).
16. Pat Milton, "U.S. Marshals still have a big role in law enforcement, even in Iraq," *USA Today*, April 14, 2007.

Chapter 7

1. Gary May, *The Informant*, 367.
2. U.S. Marshals Service, "Witness Security Program," http://www.usmarshals.gov/witsec/index.html (Accessed August 13, 2010).
3. Ibid.
4. Rebecca Day, "New book uncovers local roots of federal witness protection program," *Niagara Falls* (N.Y.) *Reporter*, April 23, 2002.
5. U.S. Marshals Service, "Witness Security Program," http://www.usmarshals.gov/witsec/index.html (Accessed August 13, 2010).
6. Ibid.
7. Mike Robinson, "Deputy US marshal guilty of leaking secrets to mob," Associated Press, April 29, 2009.
8. Kim Murphy, "One man's word against the world's most dangerous drug cartel," *Los Angeles Times*, July 6, 1987.

9. Mike Robinson, "Deputy US marshal guilty of leaking secrets to mob," Associated Press, April 29, 2009.
10. Scott Shafer, "Do witness protection programs really protect?" http://www.npr.org/templates/story/story.php?storyId=14034143 (Accessed August 13, 2010).
11. Kim Murphy, "One man's word against the world's most dangerous drug cartel," *Los Angeles Times*, July 6, 1987.
12. Ibid.
13. Steve Millburg and David Krajicek, "Death of a protected witness," *Village Voice*, September 26, 1990.
14. William Glaberson, "Live or die," *New York Times*, July 6, 2003.
15. Shafer.
16. Bill Moushey, "Protected witness," *Pittsburgh Post-Gazette*, May 26–31, 1996.
17. Ibid.; U.S. Marshals Service, "Witness Security Program," http://www.usmarshals.gov/witsec/index.html (Accessed August 13, 2010).
18. Moushey.
19. "New Mexico killer set to die in Arkansas," *Albuquerque* (N.M.) *Tribune*, April 12, 1999.
20. "Condemned Indian gains special rite," *New York Times*, February 28, 1993.
21. Moushey.
22. Ibid.
23. Ibid.

Chapter 8

1. U.S. Marshals Service, "History—Line of Duty deaths prevalent in Old West," http://www.usmarshals.gov/history/line-of-duty-old-west.htm (Accessed August 13, 2010).
2. The Trial and Going Snake Massacre, http://www.accessgenealogy.com/native/proctor/trial-massacre.htm (Accessed August 13, 2010).
3. Officer Down Memorial Page, "United States Department of Justice—Marshals Service," http://www.odmp.org/agency/3955-united-states-department-of-justice---marshals-service-u.s.-government (Accessed August 13, 2010).
4. Ibid.
5. Ibid.
6. Ibid.
7. Ibid.
8. Ibid.
9. Ibid.
10. Ibid.
11. Ibid.
12. Ibid.
13. Ibid.
14. Ibid.
15. Ibid.
16. Ibid.
17. Ibid.
18. Ibid.
19. Ibid.
20. Ibid.
21. Ibid.
22. Ibid.
23. Ibid.
24. Ibid.
25. Ibid.
26. Ibid.
27. Ibid.
28. Ibid.
29. Ibid.
30. Ibid.
31. Ibid.
32. Ibid.
33. Ibid.
34. Ibid.
35. Ibid.
36. Ibid.
37. Ibid.
38. Ibid.
39. Ibid.

40. Ibid.
41. Ibid.
42. Ibid.
43. Ibid.
44. Ibid.
45. Ibid.
46. Ibid.
47. Ibid.
48. Ibid.
49. Ibid.
50. Ibid.
51. Ibid.
52. Ibid.
53. Ibid.
54. Ibid.
55. Ibid.
56. Ibid.

Chapter 9

1. U.S. Marshals Service press release (June 2, 2009), "U.S. Marshals Task Force Captures Murder Suspect in Blue Angel Lane Shooting," http://www.usmarshals.gov/news/chron/2009/060209a.htm (Accessed August 13, 2010).
2. U.S. Marshals Service, "Fugitive Investigations," http://www.usmarshals.gov/investigations/index.html (Accessed August 13, 2010).
3. "Squatter is dragged from flames after killing marshal, aide," *Milwaukee Journal*, July 31, 1940.
4. Bill O'Neal, *The Pimlico Encyclopedia of Western Gunfighters* (London: Pimlico, 1979), 5.
5. New Mexico's Lincoln County War, http://www.legendsofamerica.com/nm-lincolncountywar.html (Accessed August 13, 2010).
6. Federal Bureau of Investigation, "FBI's Ten Most Wanted Fugitives: Facts on the Program," http://www.fbi.gov/wanted/topten/tenfaq.htm (Accessed August 13, 2010).
7. U.S. Marshals Service, "Fugitive Investigations," http://www.usmarshals.gov/investigations/index.html (Accessed August 13, 2010).
8. Ibid.
9. Ibid.
10. Ibid.
11. Ibid.
12. Ibid.
13. U.S. Marshals Service, "Operation Falcon," http://www.usmarshals.gov/falcon/index.html (Accessed August 13, 2010).
14. Buena Park Police Dept., "Darrell 'Bud' Cate," http://www.bppd.com/aboutus/inremembrance/cate/index.htm (Accessed August 13, 2010).
15. U.S. Marshals Service, http://www.usmarshals.gov/investigations/most_wanted/clouston/clouston.htm (Accessed August 13, 2010).
16. U.S. Marshals Service, "Operation Falcon," http://www.usmarshals.gov/falcon/index.html (Accessed August 13, 2010).
17. Ibid.
18. Ibid.
19. Ibid.
20. Ibid.
21. Ibid.

Bibliography

Calhoun, Frederick. *The Lawmen: United States Marshals and Their Deputies, 1789–1989*. Washington, D.C.: Smithsonian Institution Press, 1989.

Earley, Pete, and Gerald Shur. *Witsec: Inside the Federal Witness Protection Program*. New York: Bantam, 2002.

Hudson, Henry. *Quest for Justice*. Fort Valley, Va.: Loft Press, 2007.

Sabbag, Robert. *Too Tough to Die: Down and Dangerous with the U.S. Marshals*. New York: Simon & Schuster, 1992.

Stroud, Carsten. *Deadly Force: In the Streets with the U.S. Marshals*. New York: Bantam, 1997.

Further Resources

Print

Chenoweth, James. *Down Darkness Wide: U.S. Marshals and the Last Frontier.* Frederick, Md.: Publish America, 2004. History of U.S. Marshals on the Western frontier.

Ernst, Robert, and George Stumpf. *Deadly Affrays: Violent Deaths of the United States Marshals Service 1789–2004.* Avon, Ind.: Scarlet Mask, 2006. Examines violent deaths of U.S. marshals through history.

Victor, Rae. *George Washington's Revolutionary Marshals.* West Conshohocken, Pa.: Infinity Publishing, 2004. History of the original U.S. marshals in early America.

Online

United States Department of Justice
http://www.justice.gov
Official Web site of the Justice Department.

United States Marshals Service
http://www.usmarshals.gov
Official Web site of the service.

The Silverstar
http://www.silverstarcollectables.com/silverstar.htm
Private Web site devoted to U.S. Marshals Service history and collectible items.

Index

D

E

F

G

H

I

J

About the Author

Michael Newton has published 235 books since 1977, with 15 forthcoming from various houses through 2011. His history of the Florida Ku Klux Klan (*The Invisible Empire,* 2001) won the Florida Historical Society's 2002 Rembert Patrick Award for "Best Book in Florida History," and his *Encyclopedia of Cryptozoology* was one of the American Library Association's Outstanding Reference Works in 2006. His nonfiction work includes numerous volumes for Chelsea House Publishers and Facts On File.